Some Extracts From the Diary of a School Secretary

6th February At lunch time today .... of the ...... er
ladies discovered T...... Watkins behind ... toilets
with her skirt held u........................ g
the boys 5p each to .... s
Prout said there was .... h
their 5ps ready. Mrs .... s
very angry. She said .... put
Theresa up to this as the child was totally innocent of
all sexual matters.

9th February Mrs Watkins came to the office today
with £3.25 she said she had found in Theresa's
bedroom. She said she didn't want Theresa to keep it
and suggested it should be paid into the School
Funds. It was eventually entered in the ledger 'donation from parent'.

15th February Theresa Watkins came to the office
today to complain that the new caretaker put his hand
inside her knickers (without paying 5p presumably).
As we now have another caretaker on the premises no
action was taken.

INSUFFERABLE LITTLE CHILDREN

A HILARIOUS ACCOUNT OF LIFE AS A SCHOOL
SECRETARY

'THESE PIECES ARE A DELIGHT'
The Times Educational Supplement

FROM THE AUTHOR OF *HOVEL IN THE HILLS*

Also by Elizabeth West

HOVEL IN THE HILLS
GARDEN IN THE HILLS
KITCHEN IN THE HILLS

and published by Corgi Books

Insufferable Little Children

. . . being the further reflections
of a school secretary

Elizabeth West

CORGI BOOKS

INSUFFERABLE LITTLE CHILDREN

A CORGI BOOK   0 552 13347 7

First publication in Great Britain

PRINTING HISTORY

Corgi edition published 1988

Copyright © Elizabeth West 1988

This book is set in 10/11pt Melior

Corgi Books are published by Transworld Publishers
Ltd., 61–63 Uxbridge Road, Ealing, London W5 5SA,
in Australia by Transworld Publishers (Australia) Pty.
Ltd., 15–23 Helles Avenue, Moorebank, NSW 2170,
and in New Zealand by Transworld Publishers
(N.Z.) Ltd., Cnr. Moselle and Waipareira Avenues,
Henderson, Auckland.

Made and printed in Great Britain by
Cox & Wyman Ltd., Reading, Berks.

Contents

Preface

All the events described in this book actually happened (or very nearly did) but they didn't all take place at the same school and I have changed the names, sex, age and nationality of some of the people concerned. Also, to add further confusion, I have introduced a few fictitious characters.

This account was written before March 1987 when the Government published its proposals for teachers' pay and conditions of employment. Part III of the book should be read with this fact in mind.

Some of the material in sections 8, 11, 12, 14, 16, 18, 27, 33, 37 and 38 has appeared in *The Times Educational Supplement* and my thanks are due to the Editor for his kind permission to reprint.

Part I
Job description

1

When I unlock my office door in the morning – a tricky exercise, requiring a sharp kick and a lunge with the shoulder at the precise moment the key turns – I am greeted with a stuffy and unwholesome smell of old clothes and dirty carpeting, so I open the window to waft away the stale overnight stuffiness. (Opening the window is another tricky exercise. The sash cords have long since rotted away so I have to heave the bottom sash upwards for about 18 in. then lower it on to Arnolds Educational Equipment Catalogue placed upright on the one side and the Yellow Pages on the other.)

All primary school offices are curious places. I think that mine is perhaps more curious than most.

Built into the chimney breast alongside my desk there is an elderly gas fire in front of which stands a tall heavy-gauge wire mesh guard. Upon this I dry tea towels, wet socks and swimming things. On the wall facing the fireplace there is a large floor-to-ceiling dresser. The wide shelves, which a century ago probably accommodated plates, jars and pots, are now filled with untidy piles of clothing, some old plimsolls, tennis balls, plastic toys, broken staple guns, some parcels of books that I haven't yet found time to open and several dirty coffee mugs. The cupboards beneath are filled with several piles of old registers, two broken sewing machines, bundles of useful clothing (spare knickers, skirts, trousers and jumpers), the best tea-service for the Governors' meetings, and a large box of odd wooden shapes – which I

11

am told is 'maths equipment' that someone ordered by mistake and nobody wants.

My office used to be the Housekeeper's room in this large Victorian building which now forms part of the school. The floor of my office is, I think, slated. But the LEA (Local Education Authority) decided that the school office should be carpeted. It was very foolish of them. Bearing in mind some of the things that happen over my carpet I would be happier with a slate floor and access to a mop and bucket.

Alongside the Housekeeper's room is the original pantry which has now been turned into toilet accommodation for two classes of infants. Here the slate floor has been allowed to remain uncovered and the only alteration to the room is the erection of two small wooden-doored cubicles in one corner and a line of four small sinks. This room serves the daily toilet needs of 65 children who are accommodated in two classrooms; one above and one alongside my office. Access to the pantry was originally through the Housekeeper's room. But this door is no longer used and the photocopier stands across it. Children now queue up outside my office door for the toilet and enter the ex-pantry through a small opening which was knocked through from the hall. The original back door to the old house opens into this hall and as this is now used as the main entrance to this part of the school there is a lot of shuffling to and fro in the small square area just outside my office door.

At 10.30 am when the playtime bell sounds the children line up to collect their coats from the cloakroom or visit the toilet. The teachers are in firm control.

'Now line up nice and quietly please ... *Who* is that being silly at the front? ... Emily, leave William's ear alone! ... It is *not* a funny colour, and, anyway there is no need for you to poke it like that ... Now stop making a fuss William; Emily

12

didn't really poke very hard . . . Who is making that silly noise? . . . Matthew, please leave the wall display alone.'

All infant teachers sound like Joyce Grenfell.

At 12.00 noon the bell sounds for lunchtime and the children line up outside my door to use the toilets and wash their hands before dinner. The dinner-ladies are now in charge and the children, who sense a lessening of authority, are badly behaved and noisy.

'Shut up all of you! . . . Now come on, line up and stop messing about . . . Jason! Come out of that lavatory! You know Jennifer's in there . . . Come here you – yes, *you* . . . now all of you, shut up – BE QUIET!'

The dinner ladies do not sound like Joyce Grenfell.

Throughout the day children will visit the toilet, either singly or in groups. Little girls whisper together secretly: 'I like Mrs Snow best; in fact I think I *love* Mrs Snow. She's much nicer than Miss Baker. I hate Miss Baker.' . . .'Next week it's my birthday and you can come to my party because you're my best friend. But I'm not inviting Jane because she's *horrible.*' Children who come alone to use the lavatory sometimes sit there singing to themselves:

Praise Him, Praise Him, all you little children,
God is love, God is love . . .

Happy Birthday to you,
Stick your head down the loo . . .

In the afternoon children will visit the toilets to wash their hands because the afternoon classes always include a painting session and, these days, children paint not only with brushes but with their hands as well. In little groups of four or five they will walk solemnly down the corridor, swathed from chin to knees in paint-splashed aprons, their hands – with palms and fingers covered in paint – held out in front of them. But in the privacy of the toilet they are solemn no more. If you are unsupervised in the toilet there are all sorts of funny things you can do. You can run at someone else with your outstretched painty hands, going 'GGGRRRRRRRRR!' and you can do all sorts of squirty things with taps. Then there's the lavatory brush; you can dip it in the pan and then swirl it around your head and splash everybody, or you can slip the handle inside the padlock and chain on the cleaner's cupboard and try and lever it off. But – most exciting of all if you are a little boy – you can shove the brush up a little girl's skirt.

I sit in my office listening to the scampering and squealing. I let them carry on for a few minutes, but if the noise becomes a shrieking crescendo I decide I have to do something about it. Striding into the toilet I assume my Authoritative Voice: 'What *are* you children doing in here! Go back to your class IMMEDI-ATELY!' (I don't think that *I* sound like Joyce Grenfell either.) For a few silent seconds the children stand frozen and stare up at me with astonished faces. But there is always one who is quick to recover. 'It was Toby; he started throwing water first and then he tried to push me in the toilet . . .'

Perhaps the most significant fact of life in an office alongside a toilet block serving 65 infants is the smell, and it never ceases to amaze me that such tiny little children can make such abominably large smells. Moreover (and this implies no criticism of the school meals service) the afternoon smells are more abominable than the morning ones. I think I have probably become accustomed to tolerating a vague but permanent smell of sewage in the office, but when the pungency reaches a noisome farmyard level I go into action with sprays – any sort of sprays – Fresh Aire, Fly Spray or any other insect repellent I can find – even Intimate Passion or Love Me scent sprays left over from last term's fund-raising bazaar.

14

The smell is not obliterated, but it possibly becomes more chemical than animal.

A visitor to the school, stepping through the main door into the small hall will not notice the entrance into the toilet block. It is unlabelled and concealed in an angle of the wall. But he or she will be stepping forward to within a few feet of the cubicles where the most fundamental human activity has been taking place (possibly 65 times) and the first thing that will be noticed about the school is the smell. The second thing he or she will notice on walking across the hall is the propped-open door labelled 'School Secretary'.

Sometimes I get some very funny looks.

2

It was while I was trying to remove a pussy willow from a child's nostril with a pair of tweezers that the thought occurred to me that I do a lot of strange things during the course of a day's work. Children who need comfort, reassurance or some practical help will turn to the nearest adult, and as my office is within easy trotting distance of most classrooms and the playground, many children come (or are sent) to see me. Children with streaming colds and no handkerchief may remember the toilet roll of soft paper that I keep in the dresser drawer; a child whose tooth has dropped out will come to scrounge an envelope so that the tooth may be safely taken home. Is your drink-flask top too stiff to undo? Do you need a safety-pin for your knickers? Is your sandal strap broken? Have you forgotten your sandwiches? Do you need a towel for swimming? Then go and see Mrs West.

But there was nothing about all this in the Job Description issued to me by the LEA. I am employed as a school clerical assistant to look after all records, correspondence and accounts. There was never any suggestion that I might be called upon to clean out fish tanks, sweep up broken glass in the playground or bury (with appropriate ceremony) dead gerbils. And there was certainly no mention of first aid – but try explaining that to a child who has just sat on a wasp or caught his fingers in the lavatory door.

The school office is the reception area of the school and is, more often than not, milling with people. Obviously the school secretary is the correct person to receive all visitors, but I hadn't realised before taking this job just how many visitors there would be, nor how much time the children would spend visiting the office. But they are with me, on and off, all day. For example, they come into the office first thing to look for the gloves they lost yesterday; to bring me the medicine they must have at lunchtime; to collect the class dinner register; to bring me a note from their mother, or to ask for a plaster for their knee because they fell down on the way to school. Five minutes after lessons have started they are back again – to bring me the completed dinner register; to buy biscuits from the school tuck shop; to look in the lost-property box for the Star Wars figure they must have dropped in the playground, or to ask me to ring their Mummy because they have earache. Throughout the course of the morning children will trickle in and out of the office – because they were late and need to be booked in for dinner; because they have forgotten their swimming things and want to telephone home; because they have been sent by teacher to ask for some pencils, graph paper, extra bottles of milk or straws, or because they are having a nosebleed.

At playtime the walking wounded from the climbing-frame accidents will come howling to the office and a decision has to be made. Does this bashed head need nothing more than a cold compress and sympathy, or is it a hospital job? When in doubt I send for Mum. Then at lunchtime I have my midday sick parade when the children line up for their cough mixture, antibiotic tablets, asthma inhalers or eye-drops. In the afternoon the office is a little calmer, except when there's an afternoon assembly or hymn practice. On these occasions all those children whose parents object to any form of 'religious indoctrination' will be cluttering up the office, and so instead of being indoctrinated in the school hall they are crawling about my floor, swinging on my stool, fiddling with the typewriter, chucking bits of lost property at each other or fighting. They will all go back to class for the last period of the afternoon and, as soon as the final bell sounds, I am – with any luck – out of this office and halfway down the road before the children leave their classrooms.

The teaching staff certainly don't visit the office very much during lesson time. Before school starts they will give me details of the class trips they want organised, the books or equipment they want me to order and the games fixtures they want me to arrange. I don't normally *see* them until lunchtime, but they send me little notes. If the paper towels have run out or a window is jammed shut, a skylight is leaking or a dog is in the toilets, a teacher's only recourse is to send a note to the office.

'Our hamster has got out!' wailed one little note recently. '*Do* be a dear and come and catch him for us!'

The trouble with all this dashing about with messages and on errands of rescue (in between dealing with the gas meter reader, the man delivering sand and the lady who comes to teach the violin) is that I am liable to find that eleven o'clock has come and gone and I have forgotten, once again, to switch on the tape recorder. Fortunately the teaching staff (having now become accustomed to receiving from me taped schools broadcasts with the first five minutes missing) are skilled at improvisation.

If you visited me at school the first thing you would notice would be, of course, the smell. But as soon as you came into the office you would probably be puzzled by the amount of old clothes, rubbish and clutter in the room. The anoraks, cagouls, knickers, wellington boots, PE bags and plastic lunchboxes on my dresser are items of lost property – all of which have been picked up around the school during this past week. (Last week's findings are shoved into a cardboard box and put out of the way in the corner.) But if you visited on a Friday you would find my floor cluttered with trombones, trumpets and flugel horns because Friday is Brass Day and the children are advised to bring their instruments into the office for safekeeping until the arrival of the peripatetic brass teacher. If I happen to have a delivery of books or equipment on a Friday, or someone presents the school with some 'interesting' or 'useful' article, then I have extreme difficulty in getting to my desk.

In fact, most days some beaming person will come staggering into the office with an armful of something 'interesting' or 'useful'; like that bird's nest over there on top of the photocopier, and the carton containing 2,000 paper cups that will be handy for next term's Autumn Fayre. The record player in the corner (underneath that set of dental kits that are for distribution to the infants) is broken and awaiting collection for repair. All this stuff has to come to the school office because, well, there's no other place for it, is there? For the same reason I have a broken paper-trimmer, two loudspeakers and a plastic sack full of useful fabric offcuts underneath my desk.

Every now and then I have a determined sort-out. Things are dispatched to appropriate classrooms, hidden in cupboards or sent to a jumble sale, and for about two days the office looks comparatively tidy. But then it all starts coming back again and I find myself filling cardboard boxes with the latest batch of socks, plimsolls, scarves and gloves that have been picked up around the school, and finding safe-keeping places for another collection of confiscated water pistols, knives, catapults, joke false teeth, etc. Electronic noise-making wristwatches are the biggest nuisance. The last two (banned from the classroom because of the distraction caused) came in today. I have buried them in the filing cabinet beneath a pile of bank bags. But every few seconds one gives off a crescendo alarm and the other one repeats the first two lines of 'The Bluebells of Scotland'.

3

St Claude's Junior Mixed and Infants' School was an inner-city primary school built in 1874 at the edge of St Claude's Park. I use the past tense because although the buildings are still standing, the children and staff were moved out two years ago when it was discovered that the Victorian school was about to collapse – a state of affairs brought about by half a century of neglect combined with the thundering vibrations of the by-pass which runs a few hundred yards away from and below the school. When the by-pass was built in the 1960s the infants school of St Cuthbert's was demolished and the children were moved to St Claude's.

Now history has repeated itself in that the children and staff of St Claude's have had to gather up their books and move along the road to the next nearest school – Commercial Street Primary. As the main buildings of Commercial Street School were built in the last century, and have received maintenance similar in degree and quality to that of St Claude's we all hope that the Local Authority will soon pro-vide us with that brand new school which was prom-ised for the area in the 1970s, because, apart from a dilapidated warehouse and a damp and draughty abandoned church, there is now no building this side of the river large enough to take us all.

I was the secretary of St Claude's Primary School and when we moved along to Commercial Street I was able to step straight into the office of my counterpart at Commercial Street because she, very conveniently, had resigned to take another job. As St Claude's had accommodated 160 children and Commercial Street's roll numbered 280 children, this meant that overnight my workload had more than doubled. Looking after the out-of-class needs of the 160 children at St Claude's had kept me running around in circles; with 440 children now on roll it seemed that I was going to have to run a bit faster.

The events leading to the decision to close St Claude's Primary School are worth enlarging upon. The old school, which had long been suspected of sliding down the slope of St Claude's Park, was secured to the hillside by 'stabilising' bolts. That the school was still shifting was not doubted. 'Tell-tales' cemented across cracks in the wall snapped in two and the Authority did nothing about this except to fix stronger 'tell-tales'. A leaning gable-end wall was 'botch' repaired, but nothing much was done about the many roof leaks. On a couple of occasions ceilings collapsed after particularly heavy rainstorms. Then it was decided to spend some money on the school. No 'major works' could be afforded we were told, but it was promised that the school would be made safer and more comfortable. Parts of the roof were retiled, a new fire-alarm system was installed, the place was rewired and then decorated throughout.

One day, a few months after the completion of this work, Garry Rogers started a fight with Paul Bennett in the fourth-year junior classroom and as the two boys rolled on the floor together, Garry's elbow struck the newly-painted skirting board. There was a noise of splitting wood and Garry's elbow disappeared inside a small hole. The fight stopped, the elbow was extracted, and it was more a case of brushing off wood dust than extracting splinters from Garry's arm. Mr Appleby, the fourth-year junior teacher, had come into the classroom at the end of this little episode and was not so much interested in Garry's excuses — 'It wasn't my fault; the wood just caved in' — as in the hole itself. Bits of wood he pulled away from the edges could be crumbled between finger and thumb. Being a man not afraid of drastic action he strode out into the hall and took a hefty kick at the first riser in the staircase. The wood crumbled so easily that Mr Appleby lost his balance — and his shoe, which disappeared inside the hole.

While on his hands and knees groping to retrieve his shoe Mr Appleby came face to face with the cobwebby and fungal evidence of advanced dry rot. Sixty children thundered up and down this staircase daily when passing to and from the classrooms above. The children above at the time were immediately ushered gently downstairs and an emergency call put through to the Authority's buildings maintenance department. The subsequent inspection of the school revealed advanced dry rot in all floors, staircases and roof timbers. The most horrifying example was the area of floor just inside the main entrance door. A large mat was sunk into a well at this point and when the mat was lifted a hole in the floorboards was revealed. It was possible that the next child to pound across that mat might have ended up in the boiler house below.

To remove the staff and pupils from one set of premises and foist them upon the staff and pupils of another is a traumatic experience for both schools concerned. We at St Claude's didn't want to go to Commercial Street, and they certainly didn't want to have us. But, in this particular emergency, it was the only sensible action. Commercial Street had two vacant classrooms and two very large playgrounds in which could be erected three temporary classrooms.* Now, two years later, we have settled down to become one school, but the first two terms were a headache for everyone. Happily, the duplicate staff posts were sorted out amicably. The Head of Commercial Street took early retirement rather than put up with the St Claude's invasion, so Mr Masterton, our Head at St Claude's, was able to take over, thus gaining promotion from a Scale 2 school to a Scale 6 – along with the higher salary it carried. Mr Appleby, who was our Deputy Head at St Claude's, opted for redeployment and was transferred to a deputy-headship at a larger school – a post which also carried a higher salary. The Deputy Head at Commercial Street School retained her post, but again with an increase in salary because of the rescaling of the school upon the arrival of St Claude's. Mr Potts (our caretaker at St Claude's), his cleaners and the kitchen assistants were all made redundant, but were quite happy with the appropriate payments they received. Mrs Beagle, our cook, had been grumbling for years about the increasing interference of the Authority's School Meals Catering Service, and she was happy to accept early retirement.

Staff relationships during the weeks that followed the transfer were strained and edgy. Two schools, with entirely different personalities, were trying to settle down together. (The situation was not improved when the Commercial Street caretaker resigned and we had to manage with temporary stand-in caretakers who never seemed to be standing-in at the times when they were most needed.) Both St Claude's School and Commercial Street School had

---

* These temporary classrooms have since become known as 'the huts'.

drawn their children from similar catchment areas, and the children represented a cross-section of today's urban society – from the monied owners of Georgian mansions down to the humble occupiers of council flats. But each school had different policies of discipline and curriculum organisation. Commercial Street had a reputation for well-behaved children and a traditional curriculum. St Claude's (a 'progressive' school) had children with a different sort of reputation (several coach companies had refused to transport them) and there was *no* curriculum organisation. Mr Masterton – a genius for compromise and adaptability – has, somehow, in the last two years managed to combine these schools in such a manner that the best qualities of both schools have been preserved. The original Commercial Street children are now more articulate and carefree, whereas the St Claude's lot have learned a little self-discipline. The curriculum is still basically 'traditional' but each teacher has tremendous freedom within a few very broad guidelines.

The behaviour of the children in the playground is an instance of how good manners (or obedience?) can be learned by example. The Commercial Street children were accustomed to a routine of control by whistle. The St Claude's children were accustomed to no control. When the handbell clanged for the end of playtime at St Claude's the children used to rush pell mell back into the classrooms. As there was no handbell at Commercial Street School it was decided to continue with the whistle routine. The first playtime was quite entertaining to watch. It was noticeable that the children played only with their familiar classmates, but the general appearance of the playground was the normal rushing about, dancing, fighting, laughing and hopping scene to be found in playgrounds up and down the country. When the whistle went every one of the 280 Commercial Street children immediately stopped what they were doing and stood still. At this sudden cessation of movement the 160 galloping St Claude's children came to a slithering halt through sheer shock. What had happened? Why was everyone standing still?

Then the duty teacher's voice was heard ringing across the playgrounds telling the children to line up in their classes. The Commercial Street children trotted off obediently to previously arranged places and the St Claude's children, now just emerging from shock, started chatting and laughing as they shuffled and strolled towards the parts of the playground where they could see their class teachers waiting. Immediately the whistle went again and the Commercial Street children obediently froze.

'WHO ARE THOSE CHILDREN TALKING? GO TO YOUR PLACES AT ONCE AND IN SILENCE!'

It took about five playtimes for the St Claude's children to get the idea and thereafter they responded (more or less) in line with the Commercial Street rules. However, it must be said that very few playtimes pass without at least four or five boys (usually ex-St Claude's) having to spend much of it lined up outside Mr Masterton's door because of aggressive and disobedient behaviour in the playground.

Taking over the office at Commercial Street school went smoothly. This was unquestionably due to the efficiency of my predessor, Miss Robinson, who had left all accounts and records in immaculate order. I was full of admiration for her. She had obviously worked in the same state of physical chaos that I was about to enjoy and yet her official work had been carried out with competence. She had beautiful handwriting, neat figures, and all files were clearly labelled. Moreover she had left me a plan of the school and a notebook full of useful information and telephone numbers.

But I soon began to realise that there are drawbacks

to taking over from such a paragon. At St Claude's I had followed in the footsteps of a loveable old muddler called Mrs Plagg, and for almost a year I was able to blame my mistakes upon her. If an invoice or letter more than a few months old could not be found I could scratch around inside a large cupboard, throwing files and old registers about and muttering 'Well, I haven't really fathomed Mrs Plagg's system yet.' Or if it was discovered that a child in school had never been officially registered with the LEA I could (provided no one remembered the actual date of entry) say smugly, 'Well, that was a bit before my time I'm afraid.' But there was no question of blaming such examples of inefficiency upon Miss Robinson. It was also somewhat disconcerting, when parents came to the office intent upon some query or other, to notice how their faces fell upon seeing me sitting in Miss Robinson's chair.

Miss Robinson wasted nothing. Spare copies of programmes, letters or circulars, or any other bits of paper with blank space upon them were carefully sliced up with the guillotine and arranged in neat bundles (secured with rubber bands) to form pads of scrap paper for use beside the telephone. These pads are most useful and I have followed Miss Robinson's example and now make them up myself. With 440 children on roll the telephone is going non-stop for the first twenty minutes of each day as parents ring in to explain the reason for their child's absence that day, or to apologise for lateness, or to ask permission for an early collection of the child for some appointment or other. As, during this period of non-stop telephone ringing, the office is always filled with parents intent upon similar missions of explanation or advice, the notes I jot down from the telephone are extremely sketchy. This applies particularly to Monday mornings when the dinner-money tins are coming in – brought by children who also clutch loose coins to buy biscuits, or to pay for their school trip, or to buy a swimming badge, etc.

It sometimes happens that by the time I get to the staffroom during the morning playtime/coffee break to deliver the messages, the scribbles upon my pad make very little sense to me. Sometimes I find I have just jotted down the name of the child – with no further note to suggest what the information was. My comment to the teacher concerned will go something like this: 'Mrs Branders 'phoned about Tony. He's got tummy trouble – no, I think she's discovered headlice – well, anyway I don't think he'll be in school today. Ah, no . . . now I remember . . . he's *in* school, but can't go to recorders tonight because she has to pick him up early. Leastways, I *think* that's what she said.'

In an old register the other day I came across a note that Miss Robinson had written out to a teacher . . . obviously one of those early-morning messages that I find so troublesome. The note, written in Miss Robinson's beautiful handwriting, said:

Mrs Andrews telephoned to say that Roger has an appointment at the eye hospital to-day so won't be in until eleven o'clock. He will want his lunch, and so I have booked him in. He will probably have to go to the eye hospital again next week at the same time – but she will confirm this later.

The note was initialled – and dated.

I once had a long-distance telephone call from a distraught parent who was marooned in London at 2.00 o'clock one afternoon.

'I've just missed the coach,' she cried, 'and I'm supposed to be picking up Tabitha and Henry . . . my husband has gone to Holland today, and there's no one else at home!'

I expressed immediate sympathy and asked what I could do to help.

The parent seemed to think that I had not heard her properly. 'I'm stuck here in London until the next coach!' she shouted, 'and there's no-one else at home!'

I interrupted to say that yes, I fully understood the situation she was in, and I asked again what she would like me to do.

'I don't know' she wailed. There was a brief silence, and then a long sigh. 'Miss Robinson's not there I suppose?' she asked desperately.

I assured her that Miss Robinson was not here, and I wondered to myself what Miss Robinson would have done – taken Tabitha and Henry home with her and looked after them until the later coach arrived? Borrowed the caretaker's ladder and climbed through an upstairs window of Tabitha and Henry's home and let them in and provided tea and entertainment until Mum arrived? Contacted the police or social services department? . . . I was beginning to dislike Miss Robinson.

4

I have never been able to organise and follow through a routine of work in the school office. There are too many casual but time-consuming interruptions and too many emergencies. However, there are certain immovable events around which everything else has to happen. On Monday mornings dinner money must be collected, accounted for and banked. On Fridays the books have to be 'balanced'. Nurse visits us Mondays and Fridays; the peripatetic violin teacher comes on Tuesdays and the brass teacher on Fridays. During the rest of the week things just happen. Sometimes, when I'm walking to school in the morning, I form a vague plan of things I *hope* to get through during the day – I could perhaps complete the Milk Return, send out letters for the next Medical Inspection, or sort out the School Fund account — but really the thought uppermost in my mind as I walk to school is *Was there a break-in last night?*

Break-ins have now become so frequent that we are no longer shocked by them. During my first month at Commercial Street School we had three of them, and the only emotion I felt was relief on the first two occasions because the breakers got no further than the classrooms, and a weary resignation on the third occasion when I came in to find the contents of all my cupboards pulled out over the floor, the drawers ransacked and the window broken. *I* was the one who had to clear up the mess, and I couldn't even start on that until after the police had been through their fingerprinting performance. All I could do in the meantime was to hold back the wide-eyed children — 'Cor! — Look at all that mess!' — and wonder how long it was going to take me to get the card-index system back into alphabetical order again.

To my knowledge, school-breakers are rarely caught. We are always suspicious of certain ex-pupils who have moved on to secondary education and who will remember in which drawers the teachers keep money, but sometimes — when the office is broken into on the evening following a money-making event in the school — we suspect that the intruders are skilled men of wide experience. (Any resident caretaker who, in the night, hears the tinkle of falling glass will — probably — keep his face to the wall. It is a foolish man who would risk a slashed face — or worse — in order to rescue the 'Sand-Pit-for-the-Tots' fund.)

On one occasion the thief was in fact arrested and all the stolen property returned to us. The local police must have been quite pleased with the write-up in the paper:

SCHOOL RAIDER ARRESTED ON MORNING AFTER BREAK-IN: Unemployed electrician Barry Perkins was still asleep in bed when the Police moved in to No. 21b Waterloo Buildings . . .

As this raid had taken place following the PTA party and all the leftovers were still in the school, Barry Perkins had quite a few pickings, although he failed to find much money. A subheading in the article – 'Large quantities of whisky and gin stolen from staffroom' caused Mr Masterton some embarrassment but we were pleased to get it all back (along with a tape recorder, two guitars and the staffroom kettle) and our grateful thanks were not so much to the police as to a quick-witted cleaner who found a small wad of folded card and paper on the staffroom floor. She brought it to the office and we discovered that it was the unemployment registration card and a letter from Social Security addressed to one Barry Perkins of 21b Waterloo Buildings. We guessed that Barry, silly boy, had these shoved into the back pocket of his jeans and that his exertions with all those crates of whisky caused it to slip out on to the floor.

We have no safe at Commercial Street School; it has always been the custom to hide any money away in unlikely places. This surprised me at first, but upon reflection it is not a bad idea. We had a safe at St Claude's school. On one occasion it was carried away by raiders who had obviously come equipped with sack trucks, and the replacement safe (which was too heavy to shift) was attacked and damaged several times. Intruders in the night who come to Commercial Street School always search my unlocked drawers and cupboards but never find more than a few pounds of School Fund money – all in 1p and 2p coins. I'm not telling you the whereabouts of my current hiding place, but in the past I have shoved a plastic bag of ten pound notes down behind the radiator, hidden a wad beneath the carpet and put a tinful on top of the curtain pelmet. And if any breaker had visited us last week he could have made off with over £600 camp money if he had thought of looking in the size 4 red wellington boot buried beneath the football boots and sandals in the lost property box. The danger with this system is remembering where you have put it. I once spent a panicky half day trying to find the £95 sponsored walk money which I had hastily shoved somewhere the previous afternoon before leaving school. I eventually found it buried beneath dusters, polish and a canister of Vim in a cardboard box on top of the cleaner's cupboard.

If upon my arrival at school in the morning I find that we haven't been broken into, then I can give my attention to the next most urgent question which is: who is off sick? If a teacher is absent through sickness (and they often are) I must settle down at the 'phone with my list of supply teachers in order to secure the services of someone who is competent (and a lot of them aren't). In the jungle world of supply teaching the school that is quickest off the mark in the morning will get the best teacher. Anyone trying after 9.00 am is likely to be landed with the nervous just-out-of-college youngster ('I've not actually *taught* 4th years before') or the indolent yawning droop ('Well, I haven't got up yet; I might be able to get down by 10.00 – Oh, and will you book me a dinner.').Worse still, you may fail to get a supply teacher at all.

The LEA has curious rules about the use of supply teachers. If a teacher is sick for one day we are not allowed to employ a supply. If two teachers are sick on the same day we are allowed to employ one supply. If the school is without a teacher on two or more consecutive days (and it doesn't have to be the same teacher) then we are allowed to employ a supply after the first day. Circumventing strange rules such as this means my 'rearranging' a few dates. The important thing is to make sure that the Sick Return and the Supply Teachers' Return coincide absolutely.

The filling-in of forms is a major part of my job and I give all forms a lot of thought and careful attention. I have learned that it doesn't really matter what you put upon them so long as they *appear* to be correct. My forms, together with the forms from all the other primary schools in the county, will end up on the desk of a clerk in the Education Department. And I do not wish to cause that clerk any problems. I wish the forms from Commercial Street School to slide unnoticed through the system. In this way everyone is happy.

There are so many forms. I have to answer questions about the bottles of milk drunk, the dinners eaten, the number of vacuum cleaners on the premises, the quantity of paper towels we use, the number and variety of 'ethnic-minority' children we have, and how many of our new intake came from which schools, and to which schools the children who left us went. The LEA wants to know all about overtime performed by cleaners and kitchen assistants; how many teachers have attended which courses and who had time off for interviews, moving house, attending funerals or having babies. At a given time on a given day each term they want to know how many pupils are in the school carrying out what activity, and the names, scales and qualifications of the teachers. So long as I keep a careful check that the information I supply on one form in no way contradicts the information supplied on another, nothing ought to go wrong. I have to be particularly careful over the school-dinner account. I must make sure that the numbers of children and staff having dinner each term listed on my form tie up with the termly form of 'dinners served' that Cook has to send in. And I must make sure that the number of *paid* dinners served ties up with the amount of money I have banked. I will not enlarge upon the complicated system of cash versus figures manipulation which I follow in order to achieve this balance.

Keeping the LEA happy and helping to keep the school running smoothly is, I believe, part of my job. The Head would agree with this ... and he signs everything I put in front of him – usually without reading it.

5

When Mr Masterton took over the headship of Commercial Street School he was very happy to discover that one chore which is normally part of the Head's responsibilities – that of keeping the School Log – was, by custom, carried out by the secretary. It was a custom he had no intention of interfering with. My initial feelings of resentment at this increase in my workload soon evaporated when I had a quick look through the Log. Dating from the early 1920s (when this large Victorian house was taken over by the LEA) it was a fascinating account of life in the school down the years; but I noticed that it became less so when Miss Robinson took over. In page after page of neat handwriting the ups and downs of school life had been flattened out into a series of lists:

10th January.   Medical inspection. Dr Bender in attendance.
11th January.   Class 2b visited the Natural History Museum.
12th January.   Mrs Broome, General Assistant, resigned.

Now I could do better than that! Here, at last, was one sphere of activity where I could excel.

It may not be generally realised that every school keeps a log book. Pasted to the fly-leaf of ours is a yellowing copy of Administrative Memorandum No. 48 which states, 'A record should be kept at each school under the supervision of the Head Master or Head Mistress or Superintendent Teacher in a form readily available for inspection by His Majesty's Inspector' and which goes on to list the events which must be recorded, such as the absence of teachers and the acquisition of new books and apparatus. Our log book at St Claude's School was a handsome (albeit rather battered) heavy, leather-bound tome which was held closed by an ornate metal clasp. (This book is now lodged with the City Archives Department.) The opening sentence, written in 1874, made grateful reference to the founding of the school by the Church Authorities and the names of the newly appointed governors were listed. Thereafter the daily life of the school was carefully recorded in copper-plate handwriting. Some of the entries were very reflective of life in school at the end of the last century.

To-day Alderman Bagshott visited, and the children of Class 2b were able to recite to him all the verses of Psalm 121 without error. Another child from Class 1b has died of the consumption.

Other entries had a familiar ring.

Mrs Jones who keeps the cooked meat shop has complained that children from this school have chalked disgusting words upon her door.

I was intrigued by the problems of one Mr John Palmer, the Pupil Teacher, who was continually late

33

for work and sometimes absent without explanation. Complaints about Mr Palmer continue through half a term, and he finally got his come-uppance on 3 March, 1882.

> Mr Palmer arrived to-day in the middle of the morning session and he appeared to be inebriated. I have therefore dismissed him.

The disgusting-word-writers were finally caught and dealt with on 4 April.

> Thomas Flowers and Samuel Brown were to-day caught whilst writing offensive words upon Mrs Jones' shop door. Each boy was given three strokes of the cane by Mr Henry, in my presence. They admit to having stolen the chalk from Mr Henry's classroom.

But in the 1980s the significance of the school log book has diminished. I have never known a visiting HM Inspector ask to see one, and all the information they originally contained (those absent teachers and those newly acquired books, etc.) is passed, on a daily or weekly basis, to the LEA by way of their official forms. However, the tradition of keeping the school log continues, even though some headteachers don't take it seriously. Attitudes vary tremendously. I know of one lady head who diligently writes an entry in the school log book every day. I also know of one male head who realised, the month before he retired, that no entry had been made in the log for the previous five years and so sat down in his final week to fill a few pages with entries like this:

> 3rd September.   School opened with 263
>   children on roll.

10th October.	Harvest Festival
28th October.	School closed for Half Term week.
6th December.	Christmas parties.
18th December.	School closed for holidays.
7th January.	School opened with 255 children on roll etc.

It could be argued that if the school log book serves no administrative purpose, then it should be discontinued and, for all I know, some schools have abandoned theirs, but I think this is a pity. In a hundred years' time the school log books of the 1980s will make very interesting reading – provided, that is, they are kept properly and accurately. I think that Miss Robinson fell down on the job and so, since I have been at Commercial Street School, I have made a point of dutifully recording the day-to-day activities of the school. Here, for example, is a section of the Commercial Street Log Book for last term.

14th January School opened with 440 children on roll – and no heat in the school. Mr Bodger, our present caretaker claims that the thermostats on the gas central heating system have gone wrong. Mr Scott, 1st year junior teacher absent. He telephoned at 9.30 am to say he didn't feel well.

15th January Engineers from heating firm came to-day and claimed that there was nothing wrong with the system and that the caretaker obviously doesn't understand the controls.

16th January Mr Bodger didn't turn up to-day. Another temporary caretaker was in attendance but he just opened up the school and then disappeared. Miss Krantz very upset. A child in her class was sick and she had to clear up the mess herself.

18th January Medical Inspection. Dr Bender was

35

unable to attend and the inspection was taken by a young man who wore jeans and one ear-ring. Mr Masterton says he has no confidence in medical opinions expressed by male doctors who wear ear-rings. (The children seemed to like the new doctor.)

21st January The heating system broke down. The Engineers were telephoned but they said they were too busy answering calls from other schools and couldn't come to us until the day after tomorrow. Mr Masterton rang the Education Office and said he would close the school if emergency heating wasn't supplied. Last thing this afternoon 14 Calor-gas heaters arrived and were installed in the classrooms. Temperature in school office 48°F.

22nd January Melinda Barton (Class 5) stood too near one of the emergency heaters and scorched her skirt. Mother informed at end of day. She was furious. Says she will sue the Authority.

23rd January Mr Masterton attended the termly meeting of Heads with the Director of Education. Should have been there all morning, but he arrived back at school at 11.15 am. saying he had sneaked away at the coffee break. No sign of the Heating Engineers.

25th January A routine visit by the Authority's Health and Safety Officer. He said our emergency heaters are dangerous and should be removed at once. He also confiscated my office paper guillotine (the only one in school which works) because he said it was illegal. I asked him if it was legal under the Shops and Offices Act for me to be working in a temperature of 48°F. He said that every employee was responsible for his/her own health and safety.

28th January Heating Engineers arrived and sorted

out the system. They said it was 'the thermostats'. Miss Baker, Deputy Head, went for yet another interview. She has been trying for two years now to get a Headship.

29th January Heavy snow. Many children late. Mr Scott didn't turn up. He rang in at 9.45 am and said he 'couldn't get in'.

30th January Another temporary caretaker started with us. He walks with a limp and wears thick glasses. Doesn't seem very strong. When asked if he would bank the dinner money he lifted the bag (about £300 – mostly in 10p and 50p coins) and said he had an arthritic shoulder and couldn't possibly carry it to the Bank. Mr Masterton therefore went instead.

5th February An outbreak of intestinal worms in the second year infant classes. One mother blamed the school dinners. She also said that there was too much sugar in school dinners which was why her son was violent and aggressive in the playground. It was decided not to pass on these opinions to Cook.

6th February At lunch-time to-day one of the dinner ladies (Mrs Prout) discovered Theresa Watkins behind the huts with her skirt held up to her waist. She was charging the boys 5p each to look inside her knickers. (Mrs Prout said there was quite a long queue of boys with their 5ps ready.) Mrs Watkins was sent for and was very angry. She said that someone must have put Theresa up to this as the child was totally innocent of all sexual matters.

7th February Class 6a visit the Museum in connection with their project on Red Indians.

8th February Nurse has discovered that a large

37

number of children in the second-year infant classes now have head lice.

9th February Mrs Watkins came to the office to-day with £3.25 she said she had found in Theresa's bedroom. She said she didn't want Theresa to keep it and so suggested it should be paid into School Fund. Mr Masterton not too happy about this; wondered if it constituted 'immoral earnings'. It was eventually entered in the ledger as 'donation from parent'.

12th February We had a visit to-day from Mr Kaussak of the Multi-Cultural Centre who brought with him a calendar of Religious Festivals. He suggested that, in view of the increasing number of 'ethnic minority' pupils we were admitting it might be useful to have such a calendar and he reminded us that the celebration of Vasanta Panchami was coming up, also, on 20th March, the birthday of Sri Ramakrishna. Mr Masterton (who is often short of ideas for Assembly) said he would find the calendar most useful and was most grateful. He always believed in acknowledging religious festivals in our daily Assembly, which was why we were celebrating one to-day. Mr Kaussak looked puzzled and consulted his calendar. But he gained no enlightenment. It seems that neither Mr Kaussak nor the publishers of his calendar had heard of Ash Wednesday.

13th February An unpleasant incident in the playground to-day. A gang of boys pinned Adam Saunders to the ground behind the huts and Garry Rogers cut Adam's face several times with a penknife. Mr Masterton summoned all relevant parents to the school – all of whom claimed that their sons were very quiet and well behaved at home and that it must be the school to blame. Mrs Rogers was particularly critical of the project which Class 6a are doing on Red Indians.

14th February All the infants made Valentine cards to-day.

15th February Theresa Watkins came to the office to-day to complain that the new caretaker put his hand inside her knickers (without paying 5p presumably). This incident apparently happened several days ago, and as we now have another caretaker on the premises Mr Masterton has decided to take no further action.

22nd February A sudden overnight thaw and new roof leaks have appeared over classrooms 1, 4 and 6a. Cook has kindly provided us with empty ice-cream containers to catch the drips.

25th February Not a good day. Mr Scott and Mrs Snow both out sick, and we could only get hold of one supply teacher so Mr Masterton had to take Mr Scott's class. There were two nasty playground fights and one child fell off the climbing frame. This evening there was a P.T.A. meeting. Unfortunately most members of staff found they had made previous arrangements and were unable to attend. Only Mr Masterton, Miss Baker and Miss Krantz were present to represent the teachers.

27th February Mr Kaussak of the Multi-Cultural centre came again to-day and asked if we had considered catering for the Muslim children in the school by providing school dinners which included meat ritually slaughtered in accordance with Halal principles. After he had gone Mr Masterton went to the kitchen and asked Cook for her opinion. It is not appropriate to record her reply here.

1st March Mr Llewellyn, 2nd year junior teacher, came to school to-day wearing a leek. The outbreak of head lice has now spread to the 3rd year infants.

8th March Having consulted Mr Kaussak's calendar, Mr Masterton chose for his Assembly to-day the celebration of Mahashivratri (this being the night when Shiva is said to perform a cosmic dance). None of the children had heard of this before. Then (as we are now in the season of Lent) Mr Masterton asked them questions about the Christian season of fasting. None of the children had heard of this either.

9th March To-day the heating broke down.

10th March School closes for the Half-Term holiday.

These days, no one apart from me reads the school Log Book and when I retire it will probably be abandoned in one of the old large cupboards, along with the Bibles, Songs of Praise hymn books and old English Readers. But I like to think that one day, perhaps in the twenty-first century, someone will read the Commercial Street Log Book and discover what life was like in a typical British primary school in the 1980s.

Part II
School (dis)organisation

6

The heavy footsteps plodding across the floor towards my office were obviously those of Miss Krantz. There was an exasperated sigh at my doorway then in she came, frowning and angry, with today's complaint already thundering out. Miss Krantz always thundered. Her voice – a tremendous asset across a noisy playground – was less appreciated in the staffroom or the office. (It was rumoured that Miss Krantz's voice as partially responsible for the nervous breakdown of a teacher whose classroom was once alongside hers.) Moreover, Miss Krantz's thundering voice was usually complaining about something. Miss Krantz complained to everyone in general, but to me in particular.

Her daily complaints to me were often about the school cleaners; they didn't clean her room properly; they never refilled the paper towel box and there was never any soap, but today's complaint was about Mr Anderson the peripatetic brass teacher. Mr Anderson was at that moment taking his weekly class of flugelhorn, trumpet and trombone players in the Bottom Hall. Mr Anderson has pupils at two stages. There are those who can play with enthusiastic (if inaccurate) gusto the first few lines of 'The Land of My Fathers', and there are those who can produce a few loud and rather spluttery blasts. Mr Anderson was not to know that in the Assembly Hall above his brass class Miss Krantz was trying to take her lisping infants through a practice for the next infant Assembly. 'IT'S ABSOLUTELY IMPOSSIBLE! MY LITTLE

ONES CAN'T EVEN THINK STRAIGHT WITH THAT ROW GOING ON, LET ALONE MAKE THEMSELVES HEARD. WHY CAN'T MR ANDERSON GO SOME-WHERE ELSE?' But Miss Krantz was unable to suggest where else Mr Anderson could go. He needed to use a piano, and the piano was in the Bottom Hall. When I suggested that perhaps Miss Krantz could practise in her classroom or, in future, change the time of her infant assembly practice, she thumped my desk angrily with a large hand. 'But I *always* have the Top Hall on a Friday afternoon. Why should *I* have to change my time. Mr Anderson didn't come on Friday afternoons last term. What's gone wrong with the system?'

What system? In twelve years of working for the education service I have never discovered a state primary school where an infallible daily routine has been set down. At Commercial Street School we do our best. Pinned to the wall behind my desk are several timetables, carefully prepared by Miss Baker the Deputy Head. These timetables list the school's communal facilities (TV room, library, assembly hall, etc.) and indicate which class uses which room at what time on which day. To a large extent this arrangement works, but then sometimes the whole thing is upset by circumstances outside of our control. Mr Anderson's brass class is a good example. During the school holiday his programme of school visits was re-arranged by the Education Music Department and he now has to visit us Friday afternoons instead of Tuesday mornings.

Last Wednesday is another example, when a hastily arranged film-show by the Fire Prevention Department meant that Mrs Snow had to forgo her regular TV programme. Moreover, Mr Scott was complaining recently that because of impromptu visits by speakers from SWEB, British Rail and Barclays Bank he had use of the Top Hall on only three out of the six occasions that had been allotted to him last term. But then, Mr Scott is in no position to grumble about 'lack of communication' in the school. Last term he organised a sponsored walk for the juniors during the weekend when two classes were away at camp and couldn't take part, and on another occasion he took his class on a trip when ten of his pupils should have been attending a medical inspection at school that day. Teachers sometimes get carried away with enthusiasm over their own ideas; checking the diary for clashing events, or discussing their plans with other members of staff doesn't occur to them.

Unreliable lines of communication between the staff of a school not only leads to bad temper and disorganised timetables – it can also mean the waste of a lot of money. A colleague at secondary school told me that for many years the science department at her school sent out their technicians each week to buy, expensively, small bags of sawdust from the local pet shop. The sawdust was needed as litter for the cages of the gerbils, guinea pigs and rabbits kept in this department. During the same period the woodworking department was having problems disposing of the large quantities of sawdust which accumulated in the workshop. The bins were full each day and the cleaners grumbled about the weight every time they had to empty them. But the staff of the science department didn't associate with the staff of the craft and woodwork departments. They drank their coffee in a different part of the staffroom and rarely spoke to each other.

(Perhaps secondary schools are not short of money. In an overflowing skip outside one recently I saw large sheets of abandoned stage scenery (hardboard, chipboard and batten), off-cut edges of planks, abandoned T-squares, half-filled sacks of dental plaster, some part-used cans of paint, wire mesh, broken chairs, bits of a computer and what appeared to be an oscilloscope.)

At primary school we are slightly more cost-conscious. Cook always saves the empty polythene ice-cream tubs which the staff find useful as containers for crayons, Lego, plastic counters, etc., and I hand on my empty stencil boxes to the music teacher who finds them useful for her manuscripts. But even so we have our foolish moments. Recently Mr Scott presented me with a bill for £7.50 which related to a purchase he had made of a dozen 'storage boxes'.

'They're ever so good,' he said, demonstrating how you had to open up the flat pieces of cardboard and fold the ends in to make up the boxes, 'and cheap too! They should have been 75p each, but he knocked off £1.50.' The made-up boxes were almost identical in shape and size to the boxes in which the duplicating paper is delivered to us.

But the biggest spendthrift at Commercial Street School is the current caretaker – a cheerful fellow who believes in keeping his team of cleaners happy. Dusters and spray furniture polish are handed out ad hoc (the fact that they never seem to be used in the school doesn't bother him) and he seems to get through enormous quantities of bleach, disinfectant and floor cloths. When I passed on to him Miss Krantz's most recent complaints about the cleaners he was undismayed. 'You know what *she* wants,' he said. He didn't elaborate, but the next day when I went to Miss Krantz's classroom and saw her smiling and looking contented I concluded that our cheerful caretaker knew what he was talking about. The classroom floor wasn't looking any cleaner but Miss Krantz was rummaging happily through a large cardboard box he had dumped upon her desk. It contained three dusters, a brand-new dustpan and brush, six cakes of soap, two containers of Pledge polish and nine toilet rolls.

7

It is perhaps Cook who is most inconvenienced by lack of communication within the school. When an impulsive teacher suddenly decides to take a class on a day's outing, permission will be gained from the Head, the coaches will be booked and parent helpers organised, but only at the last moment will anyone think to inform Cook that on a certain day she will have to cater for thirty or so less children. As Cook organises her menus a fortnight in advance, this last-minute information is not welcome; she is inclined to throw things and use bad language. Take this Monday for example. Two junior teachers took their classes to visit the Buddhist Temple, but it wasn't until last Thursday that I remembered to tell Cook. By this time she had already ordered the meat for Monday, and she asked me what she was supposed to do with the ten pound of sausages that were now not required. I was unable to think of a polite answer.

Class trips are now an accepted part of the school curriculum. Although such trips are supposed to link up with the current class projects it is noticeable that any venues connected with 'natural history' are visited time and time again, and occasional trips will be made to places of currently fashionable interest. In view of the present emphasis on 'multi-cultural education' our recent trip to the Buddhist Temple was understandable.

'Where is it?' I asked the teacher in charge.

'I don't know,' she replied, but we guessed (correctly) that the coach driver needed no directions.

'You're the third school this week to book a trip there,' he said.

I was somewhat taken aback to discover that the Buddhists have taken over St Botolph's as their Temple – a sturdy stone-built Anglican church in the

City Centre. No more rousing choruses at Christmas of 'Hark the Herald Angels Sing'; no solemn celebration of Palm Sunday with 'All Glory, Laud and Honour'. The birth of Gautama Buddha celebrated on 23 May, with lanterns and garlands and the symbolic release of captive birds; no acknowledgement of the birth of Christ. What on earth were the Christians thinking of? I thought it was the custom for redundant churches to be put to a dignified secular use – turning them into museums or concert halls, for example. Surely He can't be very happy witnessing the opposition celebrating their outlandish festivals where His altar used to stand. Didn't He in fact put an embargo on the setting up of 'false idols' in His house?

On the other hand He can't be very pleased with the mountain of old tyres stacked in the aisles of the redundant St Cuthbert's, or the pile of super (slightly-damaged-by-water) carpet bargains being sold off at St Benedict's. But the children of Commercial Street School are used to attending a daily Christian Assembly (albeit slightly watered down and disguised, in keeping with current trends) and I wondered what they would make of the Buddhists of St Botolph's.

School outings are now big business. Just think of this: every class from every school in the country (primary and secondary) will in all probability go off on a day trip at least three times each year, and will arrange a school camp for at least one week in every year. This represents a lot of potential money for the coach firms and the organisations who have something they think is worth visiting. Early in January the colourful brochures come flooding into the school. We are urged to take the children to see a railway museum, a working woollen mill or a rural craft workshop. Country houses large and small throw open their doors, reveal their treasures and

48

install sandpits and swings for the toddlers. We are invited to travel by boat along the waterways, or by pony across the moors. If we book a special Schools' Flight we can go skiing in Austria or sightseeing in Paris. We can go ice-skating, canoeing, orienteering, or spend a day at Butlins. All these trips are, of course, 'educational'.

The organisations most likely to capture a school's booking are those that make life easy for the teacher. If you would like us to visit your collection of Lace-making and Weaving Tools through the Centuries or your exhibition on Domestic Life during the American Trek West, then you must supply a teacher's pack (including worksheets for the children) to be sure of our booking. The children's worksheets must contain plenty of interesting questions to keep the children busy ('Where was the first spindle whorl found?'; 'What was the name of the family who first drove a covered wagon through the Rocky Mountains?') and the Teacher's Pack must supply all the answers. If you happen to own a couple of acres of rough ground in a National Park (preferably along-side a bit of woodland or moorland) then don't waste it on the sheep – erect some tents. There is real money to be made from that patch of gorse, those rocky outcrops, that boggy corner where the lady's smock and sundews grow. With a bit of clever marketing, that harebell and tormentil-covered hillside where the skylarks nest will yield profits undreamed of by your neighbours. Call yourself The Penybryncoed Wildlife Park and Camp Site (or some such); have printed some notepaper headed 'Penybryncoed Education Department' (with a flying curlew logo) and prepare several A-4 typed sheets of information on the flora and fauna of your hillside. Send copies to all the primary schools in your nearest large town (include, if you can, photographs of distant mountains and close-ups of fly agaric or shaggy inkcap

49

toadstools), then sit back and wait for the bookings to come rolling in. Once again, though, you must make life easy for the teachers. You will find it worth while to work with a local coach firm and take on all the travel arrangements. You must pick up the children at school – organise several trips during the week – to the seaside, the castle and the museum and, once again, don't forget those worksheets ('The lapwing has two other names; what are they?'; 'Draw a map of your camp site and make a list of all the trees you can see from your tent doorway', etc.).

Teachers who take children away to camp or on day trips have an awesome responsibility. Although a handful of willing parent helpers will normally accompany the party these parents will, quite naturally, be mostly concerned with the comfort and safety of their own offspring. Sometimes the class returns with horrifying stories of accidents only just missed, but more often than not school coach-party anecdotes are funny.

There was the time when Miss Krantz and Mrs Haw took their classes to visit a country house which provided a swimming pool amongst its attractions. The changing cubicles flanked the pool and privacy was obtained by the drawing of a plastic curtain across each cubicle. As other members of the public were also using the pool our children were allotted the entire cubicles down one side and they had to take it in turns to have a dip in the pool. Twenty minutes for each group of children was the time ration and it had been carefully worked out that by sticking to this timetable each child would be able to have a swim before the end of the afternoon. But only ten minutes' cubicle-time was allowed in between each changeover and Miss Krantz became impatient with the first lot of children who, having left the pool, were taking an unreasonable amount of time drying themselves and dressing. She walked down the line of cubicles, thundering out commands of action: *'Come along now: get your clothes on and get out of these cubicles: you've had plenty of time to dry yourself!'* And to add impact to her words she ripped back each plastic curtain as she walked past. Unfortunately she was on the wrong side of the pool.

Then there was the time that Miss Krantz and Mr Scott took their classes to visit a castle where the toilet arrangements were rather inadequate. Making sure that all of the children visit the lavatories at convenient times during the day is always an important part of the coach-outing procedure and on this occasion the performance was taking rather a long time. The only lavatories were two unisex cubicles in a little establishment sited in the car park, but the line of sixty children was moving very slowly and, as usual, Miss Krantz became impatient. Forcing her way to the head of the queue she found that the children were waiting outside just the one cubicle. *'Why aren't you using this other cubicle?'* she wanted to know. The children at the head of the queue explained that someone had been in that cubicle rather a long time and it was quicker to wait outside the other door. With a large fist Miss Krantz hammered on the door of the unavailable lavatory. *'What on earth are you doing in there!'* she bellowed (the door shaking on its hinges beneath the fury of her blows). *'Come out of there at once!'* There was the sound of a bolt withdrawing; the door opened suddenly and a terrified coach driver hurtled past Miss Krantz and out into the car park.

The main worry to a teacher in charge of a large party of children is the possibility of losing one of them. A responsible teacher will call everyone together and have a head-count at frequent intervals during the day and a last check is made when everyone is on the coach ready for the homeward journey. To my knowledge Commercial Street School has never lost a child on an outing, but on one remarkable occasion we gained one.

It happened like this. A trip was planned for one coachload of children to visit the Natural History Museum in Kensington. The coach arrived outside the school rather early, so the driver parked, then left his coach in order to go and buy a newspaper and to enjoy a cigarette. In due course the class about to make the trip filed out from school and boarded the coach. The teacher in charge noticed, as he shepherded the children on to the coach, that a little girl was sitting in the front alongside the driver's seat. He assumed that she was the coach driver's daughter who had come along for the ride.

The coach driver subsequently turned up, stubbed out his cigarette, jumped aboard and off they went. He assumed that the little girl alongside him was one of the class. The trip to London was uneventful, with the little girl staring quietly and interestedly out of the window, and when they arrived at the museum she tagged on behind and looked at everything there was to see. It was only when the coach driver picked them up again to take them to St James' Park to eat their sandwiches that the mistake was discovered. The little girl had no sandwiches.

'Will your daughter be going off with you for lunch?' the teacher enquired. In the flap that followed lots of telephone calls were made, two police forces were involved, and the only person totally unconcerned was the little girl who said she *liked* going on coach trips.

Most class trips have a few minor disasters during the day and Monday's visit to the Buddhist temple was no exception. One boy had a severe nosebleed, the second coach had a puncture and didn't turn up at the temple until half an hour after the first one, and the person showing them around wasn't expecting two classes anyway and complained about the extra number of children he was having to talk to. Apart from that I gather the visit was a success. But I still wondered what the children made of it, and I decided to ask one of them. Ten-year-old Alex came into the office mid-morning clutching a handful of money – obviously intent on buying the playtime snack for his class.

'Can I have some biscuits please?' he said.

'You went to the Buddhist temple yesterday didn't you Alex ... Did you have a good time?'

'Was all right. Have you got any gingers?'

'What happened there?'

'Nothing. A bloke just showed us round.'

I then went on to ask Alex if he thought it mattered that no more Christmas carols would be sung in the church; no more Christian weddings celebrated; no more children christened. In fact, to take things to extremes, would it really matter if *all* our churches were taken over by people who don't believe in Christ? Alex stood there for a while, lost in thought. Finally he spoke.

'If you haven't got any gingers, could I have some custard creams?'

8

Yesterday I had a good idea. It occurred to me as I was opening the weekly mailbag from the LEA and saw the first two documents – both of which related to school meals. The first was a large poster (intended for the parents' notice board) which proclaimed the benefits and delights of school dinners and exhorted more children to take advantage of them. The second document (to be passed to Cook) was the carbon copy of an LEA order to a vermin control contractor. It bore the simple command 'Eradicate mice in school kitchen'.

Here I must digress for a moment to jump to the defence of our school kitchen. There is not a more hygienic one in the country, and our kitchen ladies have the highest standards of personal cleanliness. The fact that we have mice in our kitchen is in no way due to any neglect of duty by Cook or to any slovenly practices of her staff. But there is just no infallible method of keeping the mice away, and I wouldn't mind betting that every school kitchen in the land gets this trouble from time to time. (If you don't believe me go and ask the cook in *your* local school – as discreetly as possible of course. I mean, this is not the sort of question she would like to hear yelled across the dining room.)

The sad fact is that all schools, with their abandoned crisp packets, chucked-away, half-eaten sandwiches, cake crumbs and trodden-on biscuits are a most desirable habitat for our smaller rodents, and any mouse or rat with the slightest bit of initiative will waste no time in making himself and his family at home. I think it likely that primary schools – with all those bean bags and gerbil foodstuffs around the place – provide the really five-star rodent accommodation, and it must be admitted (although we don't generally talk about it of course) that the white-coated operative from the vermin contractor, moving unobtrusively about the school with his little white plastic dishes of poison, is a fairly frequent visitor here.

It isn't always in the kitchen that the mice reveal themselves. There was one charming little fellow who lived behind the sink unit in the staffroom and had the disconcerting habit of coming out to look for biscuit crumbs during the morning coffee break, and another one of his family had the effrontery to turn up one morning – dead – in the gerbil's cage. This event caused great alarm in the Reception Class. Was it a poisoned mouse who had crept into the cage to die? It had obviously been attacked by the gerbil – and could the gerbil thus have become somehow contaminated? The mouse, apparently healthy but very dead, gave no clue. And Jilly Gerbil, sitting smugly in her corner, was saying nothing.

Coping with mice in the kitchen is just one of Cook's problems. Another one is the Education Authority who keeps on thinking up new schemes to make life more difficult for her. A recent idea was that all school kitchens should provide a choice of menu for the children, at the same time continuing to make a profit and have no waste. (In order to ensure the profit margin the kitchen staff were reduced by half. This change in the system not only means extra work for the remaining kitchen staff but also involves great delays in the serving-up routine.) While the junior children usually have no difficulty in making an instant decision on what to have for dinner, the infants take much longer. An impatient queue will be scuffling around noisily while one child dithers between sweetcorn, peas or carrots.

The menu is chalked up every morning upon a board outside the kitchen door, which is near the Reception Class entrance hall. Parents bringing their four-year-olds into school sometimes pause to go through the menu.

'Ooh, let's see what yummy things we're going to have for dinner to-day. Look darling, there's steak and kidney pudding, or there's cheese p . . . now, come on, you can read that little word there; say it for Mummy . . . Cheese p – p – p. No, not pooh-poohs. Cheese *puffs*. Cheese puffs and salad. Now that would be nice for dinner wouldn't it? And what can we have after . . . Look, there's trifle – tri-fle, that's right. Ah, but look here; now *here's* something you like. It's a very big word; let's see if we can do it . . . Yo . . . Yo . . . *No* darling, it's a much longer word than Yuk . . . Yog, Yog – that's right. *Yoghurt*.

And you can have a nice apple as well; won't that be lovely!'

Fortunately Cook knows that most of the children will choose fish fingers, peas, baked beans and chips, followed by ice-cream or treacle pudding. The salads and fresh fruit look nice chalked up on the menu board . . . and they will keep in the 'fridge for a couple of weeks at least.

Cook is always having to cope with emergencies. There was the time when a gas main blew up along the road and our gas supply was cut off for more than a week before the service was returned to normal. With a line-up of electric kettles Cook was able to supply instant-mashed potato, instant minced beef and instant sweets, and she took batches of pies and tarts to a neighbouring school to be cooked. (I'm a bit dubious about one of the instant sweets she served up. A child spilt some upon a chair and when it was mopped up the paint came off too.) On one occasion a Gas Board official turned up to cut off our supply (because the LEA had forgotten to pay the bill) and she has also been visited by men carrying ladders and paint pots (or mops and buckets) who have been sent to redecorate (or 'in-depth' clean) the kitchen – the arrangements having been made by someone in the Education Office who forgot to tell the school. All of these unwelcome visitors were seen off by Cook with a wave of her ladle.

Coming back now to yesterday's mailbag and my good idea, I stared at the LEA school-meals poster with mixed feelings. We all *know* how good the school meals are here; we don't need to be told. They are thoughtfully planned, beautifully cooked and attractively presented. When fried onions are on the menu the mouthwatering aroma which drifts across the playground has everyone sniffing appreciatively, and the gastronomic delight of a Chelsea bun – spicy and warm – just out of the oven has to be experienced to be really believed. School meals are so popular here that we

56

have trouble in fitting all the children in. The junior 'sitting' is always clustering hungrily at the dining room door before the infant 'sitting' has finished scraping the last drop of custard from its plates. In fact, between you, me and the staff who have to cope with dinner duty, we could do with less children having school meals, not more.

Have you the remotest idea what it is like to supervise three hundred or so children who are sitting down to eat a school meal? At Commercial Street School we try to do things in an orderly manner by making sure that the children who have just eaten file out through one door, while the children about to eat enter by another. But in a hall echoing with the clash of aluminium pans, the clatter of knives and forks and the screeching voices of children, it takes a team of energetic teachers with loud voices and waving arms to maintain order. If you would like to come with me to the dining hall I will show you what I mean.

If we can just push our way through this throng of children in the doorway...'Excuse me Jason'... 'Oh, thank you Melinda'... Now here we are. You will notice this queue of children lining up at the serving hatch. What? Oh, sorry – *I'll speak a bit louder*. There's a bit of trouble in this queue. Four boys are trying to push in at the front because they say that they were last in the queue yesterday and all the chips had gone and they had to have mash. Ah, Miss Krantz has moved in to sort them out.

You will notice that there are still some infants slowly finishing up their pudding; a dinner lady over there is cutting up a piece of tart into small pieces for a particularly slow child. Some of the juniors are already eating their dinners. This table here is fairly typical. Simon is demonstrating that he can eat his goulash without using a knife and fork – he is licking it up from the edge of his plate. Oh look – Matthew has just pushed Simon's face into his plate of goulash. Oh dear, it's rather hot goulash and Simon has come up yelling and with goulash dripping off his nose, mouth and chin. All the children sitting nearby think it's very funny. Hannah sitting opposite Simon is laughing so much her goulash is falling out of her mouth. A dinner lady has just noticed what is happening and is coming across.

If we pick our way carefully between the tables we can go out by the opposite door. Now, mind that little girl – the one with the pile of plates; she looks a bit unsteady and the pile is wobbling rather a lot. I have always noticed how helpful little girls are in the dining room. They rush around wiping down tables, moving chairs, and taking back the dirty dishes. The boys usually fight. Look, Ricky has pulled Arnold's chair from underneath him. I think we had better go. Miss Krantz can sort that one out.

Let's go to the staffroom. What's that? The kitchen staff? Yes, they do look rather hot and flustered. It's all the steam from the pans that makes their faces look so red and sweaty. The nylon overalls and turbans are supplied by the LEA. Look out! Mind where you're stepping. The sausages and bits of pastry you can kick to one side; it's the spilt custard and Angel Delight that you need to watch out for. It's difficult to see against the parquet flooring, and if you step into it you are likely to skid. Oh dear, you've got a bit of jam duff stuck to your heel. Never mind, you can wipe it off on the mat outside the staffroom.

I have never 'done a dinner duty' myself. I bring sandwiches and I eat them in the staffroom. But even from here I can hear the noise in the dining hall. Mr Scott seems to be having a bit of trouble with the fourth-years. '*I don't care who hit who first – get back into line*! . . . Henry, what are you doing here; line up with the others . . . *Who is that shouting*! *Stop it at once* . . . Henry, will you please go away . . . Alice, you should be with the sandwich eaters. What? Oh, all right then – but make sure you pay Mrs West tomorrow. *Henry, go away*! What? – Well, for goodness sake don't stand there – run to the sinks . . . Oh Christ. Too late . . . *Mrs Perkins*! . . . Now look out all of you – don't step into it . . . *I said don't step into it* . . . Mrs Perkins – would you mind? No. I'm afraid I don't know where the caretaker keeps his mop and bucket; go and ask Mrs West . . . *Don't walk in it you silly boy*! . . .'

I sit cowering in the staffroom and think glowering thoughts about the Schools Meal Service – especially about their latest poster that came in the mailbag yesterday. I do not wish to tempt more children into the dining hall. It was then that I had my good idea. I will give Cook the LEA poster telling her how good her meals are, and I will pin the 'Eradicate mice in school kitchen' order upon the parents' notice board. That should sort the problem out for us.

9

They were standing in the doorway of my office. They were both very tall, and they looked rather stern.

'Dr and Mrs Twine,' the lady said, 'we have an appointment with Mr Masterton.'

I stared at them blankly for a moment; an uneasy memory stirring at the back of my mind. Then it all came back to me. She had telephoned about a week ago and said she wanted to look around the school. She pronounced her 'i's like 'a's and I had asked jovially '"Twain" as in Mark?' and she had replied coldly that it was not – and she spelled out her name. I don't know where I had written it down, but it certainly wasn't in the diary.

'Ah, I'm awfully sorry,' I said, 'but I'm afraid Mr

Masterton has been suddenly called away.' (He had looked in the diary and said that as there was nothing on this afternoon he would go down to the field with the football team.) 'There's been a slight emergency at the football field,' I added.

I offered to make a fresh appointment for them or, if they preferred, I would be delighted to show them around myself. I was lying. The last thing I wanted to do was show them around the school. People who look around our school are so *slow*. They want to linger by the wall displays, browse in the library and peep into the most unlikely corners. (One woman wanted to examine the caretaker's flat!) My working day is so full that it is my custom to move around the school at a brisk gallop. But you can't gallop with prospective parents.

Dr and Mrs Twine exchanged exasperated looks. 'I had to make special arrangements to be here this afternoon,' the doctor said. He looked at his watch, 'and I haven't much time to spare now.' (He was talking to his wife. He hadn't looked at me at all.) 'I think we had better see what we can whilst we are here.'

This wasn't so bad. If he wanted a quick tour of the school I could soon organise that. As I got up from my chair the helium-filled balloons tied to the back of it bobbed around my head. I realised that an explanation was called for.

'It's our Summer Fair on Saturday,' I said, 'we shall be releasing these to advertise the Fair and the fact that we're collecting for Oxfam. I've got to tie them to the chair otherwise they'll float up to the ceiling.'

Dr and Mrs Twine, their faces expressionless, made no comment. Come to think of it, I suppose the office was looking rather worse than usual. As well as the usual clutter I had a bloodstained bank bag hanging over the fire guard ... (the caretaker had bought some liver on the way back from the Bank and the butcher's parcel had leaked somewhat) ... and Toby Making's crutches were leaning against my desk. (Well, Toby only needs them at playtime and going-home time; so he leaves them with me in the meantime.)

If Dr Twine didn't have much time to spare then he wouldn't want to hang about, so I led them straight-away to the playground. I pointed out to them which building housed which classes and I suggested we started with the top junior classes. As I led the way across the playground I recited all the information called for on these occasions.

'Netball is played here on the school premises, but our football field is some distance away; we have a thriving choir and orchestra and we are visited by peripatetic teachers of brass and violins. The school is renowned for its prowess at chess and our best players are in the top class which we will visit first.' I paused at the entrance to the junior building, and realised that I was talking to myself. Dr and Mrs Twine were still the far side of the infants' play-ground. They were examining the climbing frame.

Not all parents demand the right to be shown around a school before registering their child there. Some still have sufficient confidence in the educa-tion system simply to turn up at the school nearest to their home and hand the children over. Others, a little more cautious but considerate of the school's routine, will be satisfied by a talk with the Head, an invitation to the next open day, and a copy of the school's brochure. Parents who demand to be shown around during the working day not only exasperate me; they infuriate most of the teachers. Those who have quiet, orderly classes object to their work being interrupted. Those who have noisy, disorganised classes are embarrassed.

I realised, on the day that Dr and Mrs Twine

visited, that their entry into the classrooms was going to be the sixth interruption that afternoon for some of them. First of all there had been that man from the LEA who wanted to inspect all the fire doors, then the lady from the Hearing Centre had withdrawn some children from classes for testing; Nurse had done an inspection of heads in five classes; I had taken around duplicated copies of a letter to parents; and the lady from the Multi-Cultural Centre had come to hear some of the poor readers.

Visiting parents of prospective pupils are not *always* a nuisance. Sometimes their inspection of classes can coincide with times of 'choose-what-you-want-to-do' and the teacher doesn't mind being interrupted. Sometimes the school seems to be buzzing with happy activity – a netball game in the playground, PE in the gym . . . and then the visitors go away stimulated, excited and full of praise for Commercial Street School. The visit of Dr and Mrs Twine was not one of those occasions.

They weren't interested in the junior department, they said. Their child would be attending a private prepatory school from the age of seven. They wished to see only the Reception, first- and second-year infant classes.

A dead starling fledgling on the Reception class entrance steps didn't please them – 'I'll get the caretaker to remove it,' I said – and a glance through the open door of the kitchen probably took them aback. It was a very hot day and Mrs Burt (a general kitchen assistant), perspiring freely from her exertions over the washing up, was standing with her back to the tall refrigerator – the door of which was wide open. With her skirts gathered up to her waist she was exposing her large white thighs to the cold draught coming from the ham, sausage meat and leftover jellies within. Her eyes were closed and there was a look of bliss upon her round red face. I tried to hasten the Twines upstairs but Mrs Twine hesitated by the menu board and questioned me about hygiene during dinner hours, and Dr Twine (who, I am sure, was sneaking another backward glance at those large white thighs) tripped over the first step on the stairs and, stumbling forward, put his hand down heavily upon a drawing pin.

I was a bit concerned by the Twine's interest in hygiene (and hoped they wouldn't ask to see the lavatories or the wash hand basins) but I knew that they could not fail to be favourably impressed by Miss Baker's class. Miss Baker, our Deputy Head, is in charge of the Reception classes and it is her principles which set standards for the whole school. The children who leave Miss Baker's class are polite, disciplined, have expressed their full infantile potential and have been educated to the best of their ability at that stage.

I sometimes think that Miss Baker despairs when she sees what happens to the children's education further up the school but at least she has the satisfaction of knowing that while in her care they have had the best start possible. Her book corner is quiet, carpeted, cushioned and cosy; the sand-and-water-play area chortles with happy activity, and her art corner is stimulating and exciting.

But the teaching area is calm and orderly, with tiny chairs and tiny tables facing the blackboard and it was from here that Miss Baker was instructing the class when I entered with the Twines.

Miss Baker put down her chalk and addressed the thirty little faces that were looking at her. 'We have some visitors children. Put down your pencils and sit quietly please.'

Across the children's heads Miss Baker spoke to the Twines. Yes, they were welcome to inspect the book corner and the art room; no, it was not convenient to discuss the class reading scheme. The school's curriculum policy was laid down in the brochure which Mrs West would let them have, and if they had any questions Miss Baker would be pleased to see them after school at 3.45 pm. A few children began to fidget and Miss Baker had to remind them to be quiet.

'We can carry on working *once our visitors have gone,*' she said.

The Twines knew when they were beaten, and withdrew.

In the first-year infants' department Dr Twine (without seeking permission) walked around the desks picking up the children's writing books. He examined them, with a not particularly nice expression on his face, while Miss Allen – who is a very kind but easily flustered teacher – went very pink in the face but felt unable to do anything to stop him, especially as she was trying to cope with the questions on Nuffield Maths that Mrs Twine was firing at her.

As we went on to the second-year infants' classes, where the plaster is falling from the ceilings in great flakes and most of the balusters on the stairways are either broken or missing, I felt obliged to apologise for the crumbling state of the school.

'But although the school buildings are in a sorry state,' I went on, 'it is a very friendly, *happy*, school.'

At that moment there came a screeching, hysterical tirade from Mrs Haw's classroom. The door was flung open and a red-faced boy came hurtling out.

'Stupid cow!' he shouted and slammed the door – which was immediately wrenched open again by Mrs Haw who came out with black hair flying, a face white with anger and a scrawny hand reaching out for the boy.

'Mrs Haw appears to have a slight problem,' I said and quickly side-stepped into Miss Krantz's room. The Twines hesitated for a moment, seemingly reluctant to leave the goings-on in the corridor, and then followed me in.

'*You've come at a rather inconvenient time,*' Miss Krantz boomed above the scuffling chattering activity. '*The children are just changing for games.*' And to emphasise the point (Miss Krantz dislikes visitors at any time) she slammed shut her drawer and hung her whistle on a band around her neck.

The classroom was a wriggling, scampering turmoil of children in various stages of undress. The sexes were mixed together in happy confusion; some pulling off their clothes quite unselfconsciously, others endeavouring to conceal themselves furtively. Jacob, who was stark naked, had taken off all his clothes and piled them on his chair and was now rummaging in his bag for his shorts, while Harry (who had not removed his underpants) carefully folded up each garment as it came off and put it on his desk.

One little girl who was modestly trying to pull on her leotard before taking off her skirt, was getting in a tangle. Another girl, with a pair of new frilly knickers to show off, was drawing attention to herself by punching the boy nearest to her, accusing him of 'looking'.

Mrs Twine was horrified. 'No changing rooms?'

There was a sudden crash from the end of the room, followed by a yell of pain. Max, balancing on one leg while putting on his plimsolls, had fallen over and caught his ear on the back of a chair. He was crying noisily and bleeding. Miss Krantz went to the sink, saturated a paper towel, clapped it to the side of his head and steered Max towards me. '*Back to the office with this one I think.*'

The Twines followed me, muttering together, as I led the yelling Max from the building. I parted company with our visitors on the Reception class steps (over the starling corpse) and from that day to this we have heard nothing from them.

Back at the office I found that Mr Masterton had

just returned from the playing field. He had obviously walked straight into a persistent book salesman who had his wares spread out over my desk. A sick-looking child was seated just inside the door and the telephone was ringing.

'Ah, *there* you are!' was his greeting.

10

In-service courses (or further professional studies as they are sometimes called) are organised by the LEA, the university and the technical college. The subjects are wide-ranging – from courses on 'The Practicalities of In-Depth Cleaning' (for caretakers) and 'High-Fibre Menus in Catering' (for cooks) all the way up to the award-bearing courses for diplomas in advanced studies in education. Between these extremes there are courses on every subject in the curriculum and every aspect of the education service which might be of some interest or use to teachers. (There are no courses, incidentally, for school secretaries or cleaners.) Every week the mail bag from the LEA will contain a sheaf of information sheets about such courses and once I have discarded those where the enrolment date has long since passed (and this usually applies to about half of them) I dump the remainder upon the staffroom table. They will be seized by the first teacher who comes in and sees them.

In-service courses are arranged in order to keep an employee up-to-date in his/her subject. They are intended to stimulate, inspire, pass on new ideas and information and encourage awareness of current thinking on related topics. Well, that's the theory anyway. A teacher attending an in-service course may, in fact, get some stimulating spin-off, but (so far as he/she is concerned) that is not the *purpose* of the

66

course. An in-service course (preferably of two or three days' duration, or one day a week for a year) is a marvellous opportunity to get away from the classroom for a break during term time. Courses with vague titles like 'Enrichment Studies' or 'Understanding Mass Media Images' are always very popular. They suggest that no-one has to work very hard, nor produce any results at the end. However, the Arts and Crafts courses are often over-subscribed (and repeat courses are sometimes arranged), but there is not usually a queue to join the Primary Mathematics Workshop courses. Teachers who are ambitious and hopeful of promotion will attend courses on Computer Studies. Needless to say, only the most dedicated teacher would dream of enrolling in a course which takes place outside of school hours.

Mr Masterton (who riffles through the course information sheets before they are taken to the staffroom) watches out for courses which apply to primary heads and he usually manages to find one or two each academic year. Last term it was a course on 'Counselling' and although I gained the impression that he dozed his way through most of it he picked up one useful tip which is obviously of interest to anyone who has to conduct interviews. For what it is worth I will now pass it on to you.

If you have to interview someone and you wish to put them at their ease (or off their guard) so that they will talk freely (and unwittingly tell the truth perhaps), then do not sit behind your desk but draw out your chair to sit the same side of the desk as the person you are interviewing. Thus, in a relaxed, matey I'm-really-on-your-side, atmosphere, you are more likely to get honest answers to your questions. Mr Masterton has found that this works, and he now spends a lot of his time sitting the wrong side of his desk.

This term's course is 'Management Issues for the

Primary Headteacher' and it is too early to know whether or not any useful tips will be forthcoming, although an ambitious start has been made with a discussion of the vexed question of the copyright laws. Too many schools are breaking these laws; too many education authorities are being taken to Court by enraged publishers. A recent scholarly and detailed article in *The Times Educational Supplement* set down in a lengthy but lucid way the bare facts of the Copyright Act, and included the surprising (to many people) information that all newspapers are protected by the Copyright Act and that it is illegal to copy any part of any newspaper.

(The lecturer running the Management Issues Course was so impressed with this article that he arranged to have photocopies made of it so that every headteacher attending the course would be able to have a copy. And Mr Masterton, wishing to make sure that every teacher at Commercial Street School was in possession of the facts, photocopied his photocopy and gave them out at the next staff meeting.)

An in-service course which arouses little enthusiasm amongst teachers (and causes great irritation to parents) is the in-service day when the school closes to allow the staff to gather together to study some vital educational or curriculum matter. On these occasions it is rarely possible for a teacher to get away with doing absolutely nothing. He is surrounded by his colleagues and the Head will be present so, at the very least, he must appear to be making a few notes, if nothing else. Moreover, if the visiting lecturer waffles on and on, the staff may find themselves staying longer at school than they would have during a normal school day. Sometimes several schools will decide to close on the same day so that the staff can gather together at one school for an in-service day.

This sort of arrangement is preferred by the LEA – especially if the proposed lecturer is an outside freelance who is likely to charge a hefty fee. On those occasions there are always delicate negotiations between the heads when deciding which school shall play host to the others, with each school producing valid and convincing arguments against the use of *its* premises for the purpose. The host school will have all the administrative work, all the catering arrangements, and the staff will be on edge.

Let me put it like this: if *that* lot come to us we feel obliged to put on extra-special wall displays of art work and written pieces (hopefully without too many spelling mistakes) and we have to fork out for bowls of flowers in the hall and the corridors. We are quite sure that our school is dirtier and more battered than the others, and we are self-conscious about our stained and threadbare staffroom carpet and the greasy marks on the backs of chairs. Whereas visiting one of *their* schools is quite fun really. We can snigger at their rather feeble wall displays (Isn't it incredible that with their modern premises and extra facilities they seem to do such unimaginative work!); we can express shock at the state of the staff toilets and criticise their hospitality (Fancy not offering biscuits with the coffee! You would have thought they could have afforded a few Rich Teas, if not some Chocolate Fingers!)

School secretaries love in-service days. (I would be happy to have one every week.) Whereas other ancillary staff are sometimes expected to become involved (a nursery assistant may be asked to attend the lectures if the topic is relevant to her work, and the general assistant will be expected to see to the coffee) the school secretary can always claim urgent and justifiable reasons which make it imperative for her to remain in the office. If our school is the meeting point of several other schools for the day then I can't be sure of working without interruption. Every half-hour or so, between course sessions, strange teachers will come cluttering up the office asking to use the 'phone.

But if our lot spend the day at another school I am left in happy solitude. I can lock the front door, take the 'phone off the hook and just potter through the day doing a bit of leisurely filing, catching up on some accounts and maybe even tidy the office – stopping every now and then to make a cup of coffee, just like any other normal sort of office. But I don't always have such a peaceful day. Sometimes I don't get the front door slammed quick enough to keep out the children – which is what happened on the in-service day we held last week.

I sent out notes a month ago giving parents the date of the in-service day, and I sent out a reminder note the day before, yet at 8.45 am on the day itself I had three children in the office. Martha Bwanta was quite defiant. 'My Mum says I got to come because I'm entitled to free meals.' But the Roberts twins were vague. 'Did you give your mother the note about in-service day?' I asked.

'Yes.'
'What did she say?'
'Nothing.'
'Is she at home now?'
'No.'
'Where is she?'
'Gone to work.'
'What did she say about dinner?'
'Nothing.'
'Where does your Mum work?'
'In a shop.'
'Where?'
'Don't know.'

The Roberts twins were also entitled to free school meals. They had been turfed out of their flat at the usual time in the morning and had come to school because they didn't know what else to do. Fortunately the weather was dry and bright so I got out the ropes, rounders bats, soft balls and hoops and sent them all out into the playground — and then sat worrying about the legal implications. If Martha bashed Darren Roberts over the head with a rounders bat and cracked his skull, could I be held responsible?

That particular in-service day was one of those occasions when only our school was involved, and a lady from the university conducted it. The title of the course was 'Communication Skills in Early Childhood Education' and, apart from breaks for coffee and lunch, the staff spent all day sitting in the Top Hall. I had a quick peep through the door towards the end of the morning. Mr Masterton, arms crossed and with bowed head, appeared to be studying a sheaf of papers upon his knee. I think he was asleep. Miss Krantz, who had arranged her chair to be behind everyone else's, was knitting. But I went off then to enjoy a peaceful early lunch, sitting in the playground with my sandwiches and coffee. It was warm and sunny and utterly deserted — no one but me, and a blackbird scratching about amongst the dead leaves in the shrubbery. Martha, and the Roberts twins? I had given them £3 out of School Fund and had sent them off to the fish and chip shop.

11

A subject of frequent discussion and argument amongst teachers is that of responsibility for the child during those minutes immediately before the start of school and immediately after the end of the school day. (By 'responsibility' they mean 'which of us might be prosecuted if something goes wrong'.) If a school rule says that the day starts at 8.50 am but a child wanders into the unsupervised playground at 8.40 am, jumps on to the climbing frame, falls off and fractures its skull, who is to blame? If at 3.30 pm when the final bell is rung an infant runs straight out of school into the road and is killed by a passing car, is it the parent's fault for not being there to stop him, or is it the teacher's fault for allowing the child to run off without first checking that the parent was there to meet it?

To safeguard themselves against possible claims of negligence many teachers take out insurance cover. To ensure that no claim whatsoever can be made against the school or any of its staff, some headteachers adopt rigid time-keeping procedures. If the school day starts at 8.50 am then that is the time the playground gates are unlocked. If the day ends at 3.30 pm then the children are ushered off the premises at that time and are not allowed back in again. If parents have been informed that this is the school procedure then the responsibility for the children is entirely theirs before 8.50 am and after 3.30 pm. If the child is killed by a passing vehicle, molested or abducted by a marauding maniac, or simply leaps around on the pavement being a damned nuisance to all pedestrians, then this is a matter for the parents or the police. The school is not concerned.

At Commerical Street School concern for the child is paramount. Mr Masterton knows that whatever rules he makes, about a quarter of our working parents will stop their cars outside the school gates early in the morning (sometimes not long after 8.00 am), turn out their children, and then drive off. Some of them will not return to collect the children (or make arrangements for other people to collect them) before 4.30 pm or even 5.00 pm in the evening. So the school gates are open, and some caring person is around the premises at these times. On summer mornings and evenings the children lark about in the playgrounds. On cold winter mornings they creep into the classrooms to 'help' teacher.

In the afternoons most teachers accompany the children to the gate and see them safely handed over to waiting parents or friends. Those left behind are gathered together in the entrance hall where Mr Masterton keeps half an eye on them until the unconcerned, sometimes offhand, parent comes to collect them. If in the meantime a child is hurt upon school premises, then the headmaster is entirely to blame. I can imagine the newspaper report... 'CHILD BLINDED BY STAPLE GUN – There was no teacher in the classroom at Commerical Street School when Mark Stubbins took a staple gun from the teacher's desk and pointed it for fun at pretty Susan Coggins . . .' So the arguments and discussions about 'responsibility' and 'insurance cover' go on.

But who is responsible for the children who are sent to sit in the office? I am employed as a clerical assistant and part of my work involves taking telephone messages and running around the school with them. No one has ever suggested that I act in loco parentis. If, in my absence from the office, a child fiddles with a power point and electrocutes itself, chops its fingers off in the paper guillotine or pulls the typewriter off the desk and crushes its foot, who is to blame? Presumably the Head, because he is the person who arranged for the children to come into the office in the first place. What else can he do with them? The children who are ill and waiting to be collected; the children who have turned up late to find that Assembly has started and they know they are not allowed to sit in an empty classroom; the children who have bad coughs and are not allowed to go swimming; the children who are recovering from broken legs or arms and are not supposed to go out to play – *someone* has to keep an eye on them.

And if the Head chooses an unqualified, untrained, quite-often-not-actually-there person, then he, presumably, must accept the consequences.

Some children spend a lot of time in the office. Some children are with me for many hours every week – just sitting around, or fooling around. Some are noisy and demanding. None of them is being educated, and all of them are a nuisance. These are the children whose parents wish them to be excluded from certain parts of the curriculum. Some of them I dislike (like Jacob who sits there picking his nose, mouth hanging open and just staring at me) and some I can't help being fond of (like Caleb who is quiet, helpful and polite, and who is with me almost every day).

Caleb is seven years old and, because of his parents' religious beliefs, he is a member of the 'Christ's Brethren in Bondage' sect. This means that he is confined to the school office during times of hymn practice, parties, concerts, carol singing and all other educational junketings (religious or otherwise) and it is surprising just how many of these there are. Caleb is not allowed to make a Valentine card nor take part in the Easter Bonnet competition (these things smack of 'enjoyment') and on no account must he witness the May Day fancy-dress parade. During this pagan performance (when the children march around the playground to the music of the Floral Dance) I think that Caleb's parents would like him to be blindfolded and put into ear muffs. (They would be furious if they knew that Caleb and I usually sit on the office table and watch it all from the window.)

Each morning, at the time of the Daily Assembly, Caleb is joined in the office by Gareth (whose father won't permit him to be indoctrinated by all that 'Christian crap') and Shakeel (whose father probably has the same view but, being Pakistani, is much too polite to so express it), and when the three first met, their exchanges of 'What are you in here for?' didn't really sort the thing out for them. They were outcasts – and didn't know why.

The holding of a daily assembly is still, I believe, a requirement of the Education Act. So the whole school, complete with staff, could with justification all be together in the assembly hall for half-an-hour each day. Who is supposed to look after the outcasts? What do the parents think is happening to them during this time? (And will they feel affronted the day they meet a headteacher who says 'Certainly Mrs Blenkinsop, your child does not have to attend Assembly; perhaps you will arrange to come to the school each day between 9.00 and 9.30 am and look after him.')

But Mr Masterton – never a one for confrontation – takes the easy way out. The children are sent to the office with their reading books 'to study'. At least that is what is supposed to happen. In fact the children soon tire of Ladybirds and turn their attention to things more diverting. Gareth likes to whizz round and round upon my typing stool and Shakeel makes for the lost-property box where there is always an assortment of model cars, bits of Lego and marbles which keep him quiet for the required half hour. Caleb, being of a more solemn turn of mind, prefers to help me. He is a dab hand at counting up five pence pieces to load into bank bags and he also enjoys ruling up columns in the exercise books I use for my dinner-money accounts. But in fact I don't mind *what* the children do so long as they do it quietly and keep out of my way.

During times of non-religious festivities Caleb and I are alone in the office. Gareth's Dad wouldn't want him to miss out on the occasion of the pantomime or the visit of the conjuror, and Shakeel is allowed to tuck into the jelly, ice-cream and fancy cakes along with the rest of the school at party time. Even *I* have my lighter moments. On the day of the staff Christmas dinner we will all don our paper hats and devour roast turkey, sprouts and plum pudding, while Caleb is taken home to eat his peanut butter sandwiches – or whatever it is that the Brethren partake of whilst the rest of us are whooping it up. And there is also the solace of the wine. On the occasion of the staff luncheon the Head always produces an excellent Soave or Sauternes to accompany the feast, and it is the accepted custom at Commercial Street School that any leftovers are the secretary's perks.

During the afternoon of the last day of term, when the rest of the school are relaxed, replete and watching a film or playing 'shipwrecks' in the Top Hall, I am frantically trying to balance the end of term accounts, and Caleb is helping. But when one is feeling neglected and left out; when the sounds of merriment and jollification from which one is excluded intrude upon a mind busy with adding up (or ruling) columns, then there is nothing like a glass of good wine at one's elbow to mellow one's outlook. Next Christmas I must remind Caleb to bring his beaker.

Part III   Teaching practices

12

When the teaching unions took disruptive action a few years ago I was working at a primary school where the Head (who was approaching retirement age) belonged to a union whose members never took strike action. He had rather quaint ideas about 'dignity' and 'professionalism' and didn't understand what 'withdrawal of good will' was all about. So far as he was concerned the most important people in his school were the children, and when his staff refused to carry out supervisory duties at dinner time he did it all himself. It didn't occur to him to send the children home.

In a school where a third of the children were entitled to free meals he knew that in the event of all children being turned away from school during the lunch period, about a quarter of them would be roaming the streets and would have no food. So, day-in-day-out, he supervised all sittings of infant and junior children while his staff – some of whom were young enough to be his grandchildren – loafed about the staffroom or went out to the pub. They were all extremely cross with him. The foolish old buffer was taking away the effect of their action and causing embarrassment and bad feeling in the school. He should have known better.

Now all of us school ancillary staff (who are not professional people and are therefore not concerned with 'status', 'ethics' or the welfare of children) have just one thought when the teachers start making politically motivated threats: how is this going to affect us? Each school is a balanced community of workers; and when one section stops pulling its weight an additional burden falls upon others. In secondary schools, where I understand that some teachers rarely come in contact with the *head*, never mind the caretaker or school secretaries, I can see that it would be possible for the teaching staff never to come face to face with the ancillary workers who are being inconvenienced. But this is not the case in primary schools.

Here we are in close daily contact. We use the same staffroom and we know all about each other. We know each others' friends, families and failings. Most of the time we are amiable and helpful to each other. We shy away from doing anything which will upset the status quo, and I wouldn't mind betting that the unions get more support from secondary school teachers than from those in primary schools.

The teachers at our local secondary school organised themselves very carefully during the last period of strike action. Precise timetables were worked out (so that no one was absenting themselves for a half-day's strike during a half-day when they had free periods) but none of their actions affected me until they decided to cancel the visits of prospective parents. We had 35 fourth-year children due to transfer to the local secondary school the following September and all their parents had been invited to an 'open afternoon' to look around the school and engage in sociable chit-chat with the staff.

It had been my job to send out all the invitations; I was now being asked (on the afternoon before the proposed visit) to send out 35 cancellations. Assuming that the union's whole idea was to cause maximum trouble and inconvenience I suggested that it would surely be a good idea for me to *not* send out the cancellations. Would it not amount to 'strike breaking'? The teacher at the other end of the telephone sounded very doubtful about my suggestion. In fact, the more he thought about it the less he liked it. And the more I thought about it the more the idea appealed.

I could picture the scene – with anything up to seventy of our articulate, vociferous and demanding parents roaming the corridors of the secondary school demanding attention; marching into the Head's study and thumping the table – interrupting any classes in session and asking awkward questions and voicing unwanted opinions.

'We must have solidarity for The Cause,' I said, and put down the 'phone. But, in fact, I could not bring myself to carry the idea through. Grumbling and bad-tempered I duplicated 35 letters of cancellation and gave them to the children to take home.

If you detect a note of sourness in my attitude towards striking teachers perhaps I should explain that it is my job to put their payslips into envelopes and therefore I know exactly what they earn. And as my monthly take-home pay is an amount roughly equal to (and sometimes less than) the sum which most of them have deducted each month for income-tax, I cannot listen with much patience to their complaints of poverty. (On the last pay-day one teacher announced dramatically that by the time she had settled outstanding debts she would be left with about £8.00 to pay for her food over the following three weeks. But this in fact didn't stop her from booking her August holiday in Greece.)

To compare the salaries of ancillary and teaching staff is, of course, ludicrous. Teachers are professional, highly trained and well-educated people and they should be rewarded in line with their responsibilities and capabilities. ('We demand a reasonable standerd [sic] of living' declared a banner one of them was carrying during the strike, 'If you can read this give thank's [sic] to a teacher,' announced another.)

81

The fact that they now demand extra pay for all those little jobs they used to do voluntarily as a matter of course is just another example of how attitudes within the education service are changing. Running lunchtime and after-school clubs, taking responsibility for certain parts of the curriculum, and sharing the chores of running the school used to be just part of the job of a teacher. In all the schools where I have worked there has been a dedicated hard-core of staff who still think along these lines. But most of them are middle-aged, and their attitudes are not always shared by their younger colleagues who demand a 'scale point' before they take on any 'extra' work.

It is the privilege of the head to award scale points to his staff. The numbers of points at his disposal depends upon the size of the school and, theoretically, he has to gain approval from the governors and the LEA but I have never known a head's recommendation to be refused. (One headteacher I worked for persuaded the governors that it would be a good thing for a Miss Plunkett to be made up to Scale II for taking responsibility for the checking and authorisation of all invoices passing through the school. This was supposed to take some pressure from the office, but as Miss Plunkett could never grasp the difference between an invoice and a statement – and was totally confused with packing and advice notes – the help she gave was somewhat limited.) And the fact that a head can follow his/her particular whims when dishing out scale points leads to some disgruntlement amongst the staff. I know of one head who always seems to award scale points to the young and pretty female teachers, and another head who prefers to husband all the points; not actually awarding any of them but keeping them dangling in front of his exasperated staff.

A wistful comment on the changing attitudes

within the education service was made to me the other day by an ageing travelling book salesman. He had come at an unfortunate time, I had told him. For one thing Mr Masterton was taking Assembly, and for another, we didn't have any money left.

'Come back the second week in April when we get our next year's allowance,' I said. He eased his valise of books on to my desk and said mournfully that I was the third school that morning who had made such a suggestion.

'I never get past the secretary these days,' he complained. 'It's getting as bad as industry now. In the old days the Head would invite you into his office, ask about the latest publications and give you a cup of coffee. These days nobody wants to know you.'

Ignoring the hint about the coffee I suggested that it was simply shortage of money which accounted for this lack of welcome at schools.

'No, it's more than that. People are getting nasty. I went to a secondary school last week where I was told to lay out the books in the staffroom. Several people dumped their bags on them and one person upset a cup of coffee over a few. No one so much as said good morning to me. Uncouth lot!'

People who complain that there are no longer any ladies and gentlemen in the teaching profession may have it pointed out to them that teachers are no longer paid like ladies and gentlemen which is the reason why they are ill-mannered enough to go on strike occasionally or refuse to help out with non-teaching duties – which brings me to this present round of unrest. If the teachers at Commercial Street School refuse to have anything to do with dinners, will Mr Masterton send the children home at lunchtime? And if he does, and the 'action' is long drawn out, will the kitchen staff also be sent home and thereby lose money?

It can be argued, with justification, that the teaching staff should not be involved in such things anyway.

They are here to teach; not to act as the LEA's clerks. But everyone knows that if primary school teachers don't collect dinner money then the system, in most places, breaks down. And I can tell you here and now that if, next Monday, there is a queue of 300 parents and pupils outside my office door, demanding change from £5 notes and arguing about last week's credits, then the office is going to be extremely short of good will for some time to come.

But teachers prefer not to upset the school secretary. A friendly, helpful school secretary can make an enormous difference to the smooth-running of a school. A bad-tempered, unfriendly one will make things very difficult. She will forget to pass on messages; she will keep you waiting several weeks for some urgent duplicating work, and she will always be too busy to book coaches for your class trips.

And so I have a proposal to make. All of us at primary school are in this thing together. Most of us are dedicated people, aware of the tremendous responsibilities of working with young people. And as we are all totally committed to the task of improving our lot, should we not all be in the same union? Let us, therefore, join together in the Union of Public Youthworkers of Urban and Rural Schools (UPYOURS) in order that we may pursue our claims in a manner more appropriate to the aims and aspirations of today's caring society.

13

Over the years I have worked at several schools and in each one I have found the following types of teacher:

Type 1.   The Mother Hen
The Mother Hen is middle-aged and not particularly ambitious. She will stay at one school for many years (sometimes her entire service) and to many children

the Mother Hen is the cornerstone of security in their lives. She can be relied upon to organise school fêtes, sports days and after-school clubs. The parents (some of whom she taught as children) bring their personal problems to her. She is a supporter of the PTA and is well-known in the local community.

She is usually rather untidy in appearance (scattering hairpins – not bothering about ladders in tights and quite often displaying several inches of torn lace petticoat) and wherever she is in the school there will always be a clutch of children at her skirts. Her classroom is homely and welcoming. The children are happy, but disciplined. (She is not above clouting one occasionally.) Her cupboards are bulging with all sorts of things not necessarily to do with education and she can always find clean knickers for a child who has had an accident, an extra jersey or cardigan for a child who is shivering, and she keeps a tin of biscuits and crisps for the children who come to school hungry. A large jar of sweets stands on her desk.

There is a variant of the Mother Hen type (the Mother Superior) who is harder, neater in appearance and better organised. She is probably better qualified than Mother Hen (who has only her Teachers' Certificate) and she is much more concerned about school rules. Whereas parents adore Mother Hen, they respect Mother Superior. Other members of staff view Mothers Hen and Superior with mixed feelings.

'It's all very well for *her* to spend so much time at school,' one young teacher grumbled. 'There's nothing else in her life but school. I've got other things I want to do with my time.'

Type 2   The Academic Whizz Kid (male or female)
The Academic Whizz Kids are highly qualified and have no intention of staying in one post more than

two or three years. They have strong views about equality/sexism/racism; will talk passionately and at length on human rights, and will drive halfway across town in order to shop at a supermarket that doesn't trade with South Africa, but they do not notice the child sitting in the front of the class with open weeping sores on its legs and a burn mark on its arm. They are members of and support the NUT and will campaign energetically for their 'rights' ('duties' are considered to be extras which have to be paid for), and will not undertake any task which they consider not to be their job. (If a slovenly cleaner leaves dirt and mess behind in her classroom the Mother Hen will get out brushes, dusters and polish and clean the classroom herself – the Whizz Kids will just complain.)

I once entered the staffroom to hear Whizz Kid Sally (BEd) going on about something: 'It's incredible! We just put up with it day in day out; we don't complain, so nothing gets done. Why should we have to put up with it?'

The subject under discussion was toilet paper. The LEA provided the crisp sort. Sally wanted soft. Whizz Kids are rarely interested in academic subjects outside their own field. A staffroom conversation once revealed that Jennifer (BA Hist.) wasn't sure whether the Vikings came before or after the Normans and she was unable to guess to within three centuries the date of the Gunpowder Plot.

Jennifer wasn't the least bit embarrassed by her ignorance. 'You see,' she explained, 'they weren't my periods. I did *modern* history.'

Whizz Kids have a familiar, easy-going relationship with the children in their class, and they like to be called by their Christian names. They make numerous spelling mistakes – 'Karen should of done better with her project work,' wrote Roger (BA Hons English) on an end-of-term report – and they don't think that this matters.

In their spare time Whizz Kids read nothing but the job vacancy pages of *The Times Educational Supplement*. They rarely attend PTA meetings and when the going-home bell rings at the end of the day they are out of the school gates almost before the children.

Type 3 The Chaos Causers (male or female)

Not all teachers have the ability to control a class of lively children. Some would-be teachers are surprised to discover – usually during their first teaching practice – that they do not have this ability. (A termly drama in most schools is that of the student teacher weeping in the staffroom.) Some give up at this stage and leave the profession to seek less demanding work; others persist and struggle on.

The sensitive ones who continue to battle with a class of children will probably have a nervous breakdown after about eighteen months. The clever ones will side-step in their careers to become educational psychologists or educational administrators – professions which are known to be havens for failed teachers.

Now the Chaos Causers are cheerful, enthusiastic teachers who are totally incapable of controlling *two* children together, never mind a whole class of them – *but they do not realise it*. If a Chaos Causer takes over a class of docile and obedient children he will, in the space of three days, turn them into an hysterical, screeching mob of lunatics and he will thoroughly enjoy himself in the process.

A female Chaos Causer was once appointed to my school. She was in her thirties, attractive and very smart in a bejewelled sort of way, highly qualified, enthusiastic and articulate. According to her curriculum vitae she had taken children camping, canoeing and sailing; had run craft courses and organised drama workshops and appeared to offer all the skills, talents and energy that any headteacher could want.

In the week following her appointment I passed her

classroom and heard a most appalling noise going on inside. Assuming that there was no teacher in charge I opened the door and looked in. Mrs Chaos Causer was seated at her desk in earnest conversation with a child standing beside her and with an exercise book open on the desk between them. Another child, with its hands on the back of her chair, was leaping up and down behind her; two children in front were playing with the pencil sharpener on her desk, and a queue of children – all with exercise books – were lined up alongside. They were arguing, jostling and shouting. The rest of the class were throwing books across the room or leaping about on top of the desks.

At breaktime Mrs Chaos Causer came down to the staffroom smiling serenely. 'We've had a most *interesting* morning,' she said.

A male Chaos Causer I know has just retired after serving twenty years in the same school. Each year, thirty or so children have spent three terms in his classroom, during which time most of them became badly behaved, some of them were physically injured, and few of them learned anything worthwhile. When he was on lunch duty the dining room was a shambles; when he was on playground duty at least two or three children were hurt. Other teachers dreaded sharing coach journeys with him. But now he has retired. He has a benign and unlined face, a trim figure and he looks a decade younger than his 65 years. During all his school career he lost no time at all through sickness; during the same period two of his headteachers took early retirement and another, who had a stroke, didn't make it.

Type 4   The Chip Carriers (male or female)
Chip Carriers are middle-aged and excellent teachers (in the traditional way) who feel that they have not gained the promotion they deserve. Some of them carry their chip very lightly (and only the occasional

sarcastic remark in the staffroom will reveal their feelings) but some complain continually and become staffroom bores. Other members of staff feel sorry for the Chip Carriers and so make allowances for them – which is just as well because some of them develop peculiar habits.

Female Chip Carriers are sometimes hysterical and they become obsessed with trivialities. I knew one who attached great importance to a rubber band. Each day the dinner-money tin would arrive at my office with its lid held in place with a rubber band. The child carrying the tin always had a little note to give me. The note said, 'Please may I have the rubber band back.' Each day I emptied the tin of money, placed the band inside the tin and handed it back to the child.

One day the band broke, so I threw it away. Within two minutes of the child leaving my office he was back again with another note – this time written in red Biro – 'Please may I have my rubber band back.' I was tempted to fish the broken band from my waste-paper basket and give it to the child but instead I found another one to replace it. But the child returned once more and handed me back the band with yet another note – this time written in block capitals, with some words underlined for emphasis. 'THIS IS <u>NOT</u> MY RUBBER BAND. MY BAND WAS BLUE AND <u>MUCH WIDER</u> THAN THIS ONE.'

The same teacher became very upset once when I lost her Trip Money tin. I offered her an old Elasto-plast tin as replacement, or a floral biscuit tin, but she was not at all happy.

'*My* tin was a Mackintosh's Toffee tin and it had a *special mark* on the lid,' she said, and insisted that a child be sent around all the classes with a note in an effort to find it.

When her coffee mug went missing for a few days she was furious and put up on the staffroom wall a huge notice written in thick black felt-tip pen, 'WILL THE PERSON WHO HAS <u>STOLEN</u> MY MUG PLEASE RETURN IT <u>IMMEDIATELY</u>.'

Male Chip Carriers sometimes become bitter and devious and are frequently to be found prowling around the school after everyone else has gone home.

'Oh, I was just coming in to check that the photocopier was switched off'' said one who was surprised to find me doing a bit of overtime in the office late one afternoon.

When I knew he was going to organise an after-school club I always had to remember to lock all drawers and cupboards in the office otherwise things would be missing the next day.

Sometimes items of lost property would vanish.

'Have you seen my navy-blue Guernsey?' a child came to ask one day.

'Yes, it's right there on top . . .' But it wasn't. A few moments ago the Guernsey had been on top of the pile, but now it had gone. Then I remembered leaving the office with a pile of letters to distribute. I had passed the Chip Carrier on his way in.

'Just going to 'phone up St Jude's to arrange a match,' he said.

Clothing which vanished inexplicably from my Lost Property box was always of good quality; and always of a size that would fit the Chip Carrier's own children. When boxes of cassette tapes disappeared from the stockroom and when calculators and a radio/tape recorder went missing we all suspected him. Everyone knew what he was up to.

We think he suffered from a sense of injustice – 'After all I've done for this school I'm entitled to get a bit back when I can,' is probably how he reasoned it out to himself.

Female Chip Carriers also sometimes help themselves to other people's property but there is no reasoning behind their actions. (You must remember that many of them are coping with the menopause.) I knew one, Mrs X, who had a very large pine cupboard in her room which she always kept locked. If any adult approached her whilst she was scratching about in her cupboard she always slammed the door shut and locked it.

One day when she was absent because of sickness, the Deputy Head borrowed several bunches of keys from the caretaker and, with the somewhat bewildered connivance of the supply teacher, he tried them all out until he found a key to fit the cupboard lock. Inside, along with an unnecessarily large stock of exercise books, rulers, pencils and crayons, he found the xylophone, four recorders and a drum (all of which had disappeared from the music room some months previously), a large earthenware vase (from the staff room) and a complete set of medical notes for fifteen children who had attended a medical inspection the year before. (I remembered the occasion well. I had spent an entire morning searching for them because I *knew* I had put them on my side table ready for collection by Nurse.)

The discovery of this key made life a little easier for us. Subsequently, when any article went missing, I would wait until Mrs X had taken her class swimming or to the playing field, then I would go and open her cupboard. Quite often the missing item was there — and a few others that hadn't yet been missed. I would remove them all, relock the cupboard and hand back the property to the owners.

We never challenged Mrs X. No mention had been made of the rescued musical instruments, nor the staff room vase which was restored to its normal place on the table. We noticed no change in Mrs X's demeanour. The peculiar thought-processes which triggered off her thefts obviously went into reverse in order for her to accept the incidences of disappearing items from her cupboard.

Type 5   The Good Sort (mostly female)

The Good Sort is the type of teacher that every Head wants on his supply list ('*Marvellous* girl, Miss Bungullop – so reliable – always available – always turns up early, well prepared and happily takes on dinner and playground duties – *lovely* girl') but no head is keen to have her on his permanent staff ('Oh dear; Miss Bungullop has applied for our Fixed Term Contract vacancy. How embarrassing; I mean – she's a lovely girl, a real *good sort* but, well, no *flair*, no *imagination* – and that *voice*! I don't think I could put up with that every day in the staff room.')

The Good Sort comes from a humble background, speaks with a strong local accent and, if she is single, lives with her parents who are very proud of her. If she is young she will suffer from the same disability as the Whizz Kids (unable to spell or write grammatically correct English) but, unlike them, she is worried about this. When the Good Sort writes out letters of application for permanent teaching posts she will do so with the dictionary open beside her.

But although she may be called for interviews she is at a disadvantage as soon as she is confronted by the interviewing panel. Worried and nervous, she will sit stolidly in her chair clutching her handbag upon her knees and answering questions in monosyllables, and the job will go to a jolly Whizz Kid who prances into the office with flouncing hair and sparkling eyes and, with hands waving about, will impress the governors with her animated talk of pursuing an integrated day in a team-teaching family group situation following the High Scope cognitatively orientated curriculum . . . etc.

A Good Sort who secures a permanent post will go out of her way to be helpful to other members of staff but if she enters into any general staffroom conversation she will usually preface her remarks with a comment such as 'What I always say is . . .' and will then voice an absolutely predictable opinion. She will listen to a counter-argument with a blank face, then repeat what she had previously said, only louder.

But whereas the Good Sort often finds relationships with adults difficult and unfruitful, her communication with children is warm, stimulating and rewarding – both to them and her. In front of her class she is articulate, enthusiastic and inspiring. But if the Head walks in she will go to pieces. Left to her own devices she will take the children through the curriculum carefully and thoughtfully and they respond by working well. Yet she dreads open evenings and confrontations with parents. Even more she dreads the thought of having a student placed in her class for 'observation' or 'teaching practice'. A Good Sort will remain in the same post for many years, serving her school faithfully. She will not seek promotion and may, eventually, turn into a Mother Hen.

To generalise, I consider that there is a touch of the Mother Hen compassion in most female teachers, and a streak of the Whizz Kid arrogance in most male teachers. But the ability to *teach* is a gift. Some of them have it, and some have not. One young man I once knew was highly qualified, intelligent, good-looking, athletic, fond of children and desperately anxious to make a career from teaching. But he couldn't control his class and seemed incapable of stimulating the children's imagination or encouraging them to work. Every time I went into his room I found him waving his arms about and bawling at the top of his voice whilst the children, largely ignoring him, went about their own noisy and boisterous affairs.

In the same school was a girl who was in charge of an older and even more boisterous year-group. When she was out of the room the children rushed about, shouted and threw things at each other, but as soon as she entered they would scurry back to their desks and prepare to work. She had perfect control without ever raising her voice and she had captured the children's interest.

Within earshot of my office there is an infant class whose daily activities form a background murmur to my work. I can hear them answering questions, I can hear the general buzz when they are working in groups and sometimes, when they are singing, I hum along with them. But when a period of general activity is to be followed by a period of listening to teacher I hear the class brought to a halt by the sound of teacher's voice ringing out 'Everybody STOP' – and everybody does. There is immediate silence.

One day I went into the classroom and found that teacher wasn't there. The sound of a flush being pulled at the end of the corridor suggested the reason for her absence but, in the meantime, the class was becoming rather noisy. But I knew exactly what to do. It was easy.

'Everybody STOP' I yelled.

There was a slight lessening of noise from the half a dozen or so children scrambling about on the floor at my feet and they looked up at me in astonishment. From the expressions on their faces they had obviously come to the conclusion that Mrs West had gone mad, whereupon they turned away and carried on shouting at each other. The rest of the class totally ignored me. This gift, this mysterious ability to charm children into obedience is, I am convinced, a talent that cannot be taught or learned. And it's obvious that I haven't got it.

A headteacher interviewing candidates for a vacant post in his school must be almost as nervous as the applicants sitting before him. He knows that a bad teacher, no matter how well qualified, is useless; and a good teacher, even if semi-literate, is priceless –

and he may have to live with his decision for a very long time. It is easy to appoint a new teacher; the head simply writes to the LEA and tells the Director of Education of his choice. But, once appointed, it is almost impossible to get rid of one.

14

Teachers with ambition used to work their way up the Scales in the hope of becoming deputy head, intending eventually to become Headteacher of their own school. I understand that these days less of them are seeking the final rung of the ladder and that in some inner-city areas headships have remained vacant – the schools being run by temporary 'task force' heads. The job of primary school headteacher is a curious one. In order to have been chosen for the job in the first place he/she would have been able to offer many years of experience, would have been highly thought of by his/her superiors and, probably, would have worked hard in order to obtain some academic qualification. But none of these attributes is of much help when actually *doing* the job. In order to survive as headteacher a man or woman must have many talents – few of which have much connection with education.

Mr Masterton, Head of Commercial Street School is, I think, fairly typical. Now in his mid-fifties he is Head of a large school and is at the top of his career. He can go no further. Being a man aware of the importance of always gauging current trends he has attended all appropriate in-service courses and, when in his late forties, even made the effort to obtain a degree (BA in Sociology, Open University). But how does he spend his days at school? Yesterday was a good example, and I made a few notes about it.

8.15 am

Head arrives to find window of his office broken by overnight intruders who have ransacked his desk. I help him to clear up mess.

8.50 am

Two parents wish to see Head, also Police arrive to discuss break-in.

9.30 am

Assembly – which was to have been a BBC school's broadcast but which Head has to improvise hastily because overnight intruders stole radio.

9.50 am

Head settles in office to sort out next term's class lists.

10.10 am

I interrupt him to tell him that the kettle has 'gone wrong' and staff will be wanting their coffee at 10.30 am. Head examines kettle, traces fault to plug and swaps the plug from his electric fire to the kettle.

11.05 am

After playtime Head returns to the class lists but has to abandon them as a child has fallen from a piece of equipment in the gymnasium and appears to be concussed. Parents cannot be contacted so Head takes child to Casualty Department of hospital.

1.45 pm

Head returns from hospital, having handed over care of child to parents who have now been traced. Head sits down to warmed-up lunch.

2.10 pm

Head resumes work on class lists.

2.15 pm

I interrupt him to tell him that the games coach has not turned up so Head and games master use their cars to ferry boys to football field.

2.35 pm

Head returns to find water flowing from the boys' toilets. As this is the caretaker's 'stand-down' time Head investigates; rolls up his sleeve, and removes toilet rolls blocking lavatory pans.

2.50 pm

Head signs some letters, makes a couple of telephone calls and then returns to class lists.

3.05 pm

Head abandons class lists in order to go to games field and collect boys.

3.25 pm

Head returns to find caretaker complaining that he cannot attend to large broken window in Head's room without help.

3.45 pm

As I leave school Head is standing on stepladder holding large piece of hardboard in place over broken window pane while caretaker fixes it. I understand that after I have left a mother comes to complain that her child is being victimised by a teacher, a little old lady who has been knocked down outside the school is brought in to the office to recover, and an angry park attendant, waving a muddy rake, storms in to say that some of our fourth-year boys who have just run out of the school are now tearing up tulips in the park.

5.00 pm

Mr Masterton is still in school with three children who have not yet been picked up by their parents.

I wonder how many headteachers hold on to their jobs until the age of 65? I gather from Mr Masterton that the discussions at area heads' meetings are less concerned with matters of curriculum, staffing and policy than the exchange of gossip on the latest stroke/heart attack/mental breakdown victim among their ranks and which of the remainder will be applying for early retirement.

Some local authorities, overwhelmed by the number of such applicants, have withdrawn the option from all but the most pressing cases. Under these circumstances a man, say, in his fities, still sane and wishing to leave while he still has health and energy, will have to think up some devious reason to persuade the LEA to release him.

One sure way is to write a lengthy, controversial article on matters of racial concern and get it published in a right-wing magazine. The LEA will have you out (sometimes with generous terms) before the end of the academic year.

Alternatively you can confess to some sexual aberration. It is rumoured in this area that one man, whose application for early retirement was turned down, gained an immediate reversal of this decision by writing to the Director of Education expressing concern for the safety of the children in his care; 'I find myself irresistibly drawn towards the little boys . . . I just can't stop myself fondling them.'

Mr Masterton has no plans for early retirement. He is, he claims, a survivor.

'All you need is stamina and a knack of developing the *right attitude* to all problems.'

We were having this discussion over an afternoon cup of tea during a brief but peaceful respite. The day had been full of surprises. Mr Masterton had known, as he drove into work that morning, that the day ahead was going to be a busy one. The Health Authority team of dentists was coming to carry out their annual inspection of teeth; he had a meeting arranged at 11.00 am with contractors who wished to discuss the digging-up of the playground to lay new soil pipes to the main sewer, and he simply had to finish the report for the next Governors' Meeting because the damned thing should have been posted yesterday.

Moreover he'd better get the new gymnasium equipment ordered or Miss Krantz would be nagging him again, but before he did anything else he must, first thing, ring the Social Services about the Bennett girl because she ought to be put on the 'At Risk' Register.

All these problems were being thought about by Mr Masterton as he was driving to work. He should have been concentrating upon his driving. He told me that he was still thinking about the Bennett girl when there was a sudden jolting crash and he found himself crunched into the back of the car in front.

'Well, the bloody fool started to pull into the roundabout then he stopped!'

This meant of course that Mr Masterton was half-an-hour late for work and he found on arrival that he had immediately to take charge of Mr Scott's class. (Mr Scott had telephoned to say he had a 'tummy upset' and the supply teacher I had booked hadn't yet arrived.)

The morning meeting with the sewerage contractors had raised more problems than it solved. The contractors were insisting that the work had to be done before the end of the financial year (otherwise the LEA might cancel it); Miss Baker the Deputy Head was insisting that the work couldn't be done during term time because the open trenches could not be safely fenced from the children; and the caretaker declared he had instructions from his union not to open the school to anyone during the holidays.

During dinner-hour play a child pulled a loose stone from one of the playground walls. The stone was a heavy one and the child's foot was crushed.

'I've been meaning to get something done about that wall for a long time.' (Mr Masterton was biting his lip as he said this.) The father of the child with the crushed foot was something 'high up' in ITV. 'He'll have the bloody cameras down here – doing a feature on "Safety in our Schools".'

It was after this event that I had made us both a mug of tea. It was now 2.15 pm and the school was, for the moment, quietly working and Mr Masterton had a chance to check over to himself, and to me, the things still to be done. He would have to put the car in for repair; could he manage without it tomorrow? No, damn, he'd promised to take a party of children to a musical event at another school. He'd have to write the Governors' report at home tonight . . . and he *still* hadn't telephoned Social Services about the Bennett girl.

'What's more,' he said, fingering his eyelid, 'I think I've got a stye coming.'

It was then we had come to the subject of early retirement.

'Survival is, as I have said, a question of having the *right attitude*,' Mr Masterton insisted. 'You just mustn't let these things affect you. For example, I'm just not going to worry about that stone falling out of the wall. Worry is stress – that's the killer. Just take each day as it comes; do the best you can – and don't worry about what doesn't get done. I can tell you – the job's not going to get *me* down. *I'm* not going to become stressed.' (The telephone started to ring.) 'I am *not* going to get *stressed*! (He banged down his mug and stood up.) I AM NOT GOING TO GET STRESSED!'

And as he left the office he gave the door a thunderous kick.

15

'There's a bird in my room,' said Mr Masterton. 'Will you go and get it out for me?' He was standing in the office doorway, his hands waving vaguely in front of his chest, his fingers twitching with distaste. In his role of headmaster he is prepared to tackle many humble and sometimes unpleasant jobs. I have known him grab the caretaker's mop and bucket to swab down the floor in the dining hall when someone was sick, and he has also been known to hastily clean the infants' hand-washbasins when an important visitor was due. But he can never bring himself to handle a live and fluttering bird.

Mr Masterton is not the only member of staff who is squeamish about wild creatures and when Sandy Baker took a slow worm into class to show his friends I received an urgent note from his teacher. 'We've got a snake thing here, *please* could you come and do something about it!'

Sandy had found the creature among the long rough grass of the derelict warehouse site alongside the school and when I got to the classroom I found that Sandy had dropped it into his lunch box and was trying to persuade it to eat broken biscuits and crisps. I explained that slow worms wouldn't live long on such a diet and that it would be better if I took it outside to the rough grass again. Sandy didn't argue. Once he had discovered that it was a worm and not a snake he had lost interest.

The acre or so of waste land alongside the school is a tangle of buddleia, elder and bramble, with stands of ragwort, rose bay willow herb, valerian and moon-daisies amongst the grass. So it is not unusual for birds and animals to find their way into school. I once had to rescue a tiny shrew from a corridor, and on another occasion I went into the staffroom to find an elephant hawk moth fluttering at the window where two members of staff with rolled-up newspapers were hysterically attacking it.

However, while most of the Commercial Street School staff have a fervent dislike of physical contact with wildlife they all feel it is a subject in which the children should be encouraged to take an interest. Natural history television documentaries are watched and tape-recorded; bird, butterfly and flower identification books fill our library shelves, and the summer school trips will usually have a wild-life theme.

But the scrubby piece of overgrown land beside the school is ignored. Here, throughout the spring, summer and autumn, in and around the fallen pock-marked walls, the long grass and undergrowth, many things are born, feed, grow and die unobserved. No one notices the pied wagtails to-ing and fro-ing their nest in the wall; the goldfinches feed uninterrupted upon the seeding thistle heads, and the red admirals, commas, small tortoishell and peacock butterflies dance unseen over the flowers in the grass. Meanwhile the children are taken for long coach rides to visit Butterfly Farms, Bird Sanctuaries and Nature Trails. Whatever the subject of the current class project it will be linked, albeit somewhat tenuously, with a wild life visit.

I have never really come to terms with the speed at which class projects are taken up, followed with enthusiasm and then abandoned. Wool and weaving were being investigated during my first term as a school secretary and I was most impressed with the display in one of the infant classrooms. Pictures and diagrams covered the walls, showing the whole process of weaving from the shorn sheep to the finished article.

A lady visited the class once or twice to demonstrate the spinning wheel, and each child was busy with a little weaving frame and coloured wools.

'I've got a bundle of raw wool at home,' I said to the teacher. 'Perhaps the children would like to use it to try carding the wool or maybe even using a spindle and whorl; I've also some samples of Welsh tapestry weaving – and quite a few books on the history of the woollen industry . . . Would you like me to bring a few things in?'

Teacher was delighted. 'That's absolutely marvellous, simply super!'

What I didn't realise was that she wanted it all *tomorrow*. Over the next couple of weeks I sorted out some of my books, found the wool and, during the holiday, looked out some pieces of tapestry cloth. When I took it all in to school and carried it into the classroom the teacher looked at it in astonishment.

'But that was *last* term,' she said. 'This term we're doing electricity.'

Class projects are wide-ranging and sometimes very ambitious. At Commercial Street School Greek Civilisation (dealt with in seven weeks) was followed by Our Body and How It Works, and the academic year ended with Water. It is not necessary for a teacher to know anything about the chosen subject (books can be taken from the library; exhibits borrowed from the museum loan service) nor need the teacher be particularly interested.

One teacher whose class did a project on Animals and Insects That Are Useful detested everything that crawled, wriggled or buzzed and she kept two kinds of aerosol insect-killer in her classroom. A parent who had co-operated by providing the class with tadpoles offered her several little frogs to let loose in her garden at home, with the suggestion that they would help to keep down garden pests.

She shuddered at the thought. 'I can't bear frogs,' she said, 'I'd rather use slug poison thank you.'

Another teacher, whose project was Nutrition and the Food We Eat had the whole class making wholemeal bread and writing pompous little pieces about the benefits of a wholesome additive-free diet. Yet her own lunch usually consisted of a can of Diet Pepsi and supermarket sausage rolls.

'Don't let the children know I'm eating this,' she once said during that particular term. She was munching her way through a supermarket scotch egg and, in between mouthfuls, she read out the list of ingredients on the wrapper. In addition to the egg, pork, 'cereal' and breadcrumbs there were colours E102, E127 and 2G, Caramel E150, stabilisers E412 and E466 and emulsifier E450.

But if the teachers' attitudes to their projects are sometimes tongue-in-cheek, the children usually respond with innocent enthusiasm and an accompanying Natural History outing is always woven happily into the theme. The Commercial Street children linked their project on Our Gas Supply with a visit to the Arboretum; and the project on People in the Community Who Help Us included a visit to the Cotswold Farm Park. Almost all children, whatever their background or abilities, are interested in plants and animals.

The bird flapping about in Mr Masterton's room was a young jackdaw. I finally trapped it in the curtains and, closing my hands over its wings, I carried it from his room and along the corridor to the outside door. A boy coming from the toilets stood and watched me approach – a broad grin spreading over his face.

'Look,' I said. 'This is a jackdaw.'

It occurred to me that the child had never seen a jackdaw close up. Perhaps a jackdaw to him was just another black bird flying around the chimney pots. He could now see the bird's light grey mantle and blue eyes.

'Hasn't he got a nice expression,' I said.

'Yes,' said the boy, grinning wider still, 'and he's done a dirty all down your skirt.'

16

Our new cleaner (who is paid £1.8026 per hour for 14.47 hours per week) is a hard-working woman of mature years who left school in 1939 and has never since entered a state primary school; leastways not until she started work with us last term. Having received the benefit of a state education which was then termed 'elementary', she is totally out of date with modern attitudes, concepts and opportunities and is completely baffled by much of what she sees in the classrooms that she cleans.

She knows that the LEA is desperately short of money (she has read this in the newspaper) and so she retrieves from wastepaper baskets any half-filled exercise books, blank sheets of paper or abandoned pencils, and carefully piles them upon the teacher's desk. But of most concern to her is what she sees written upon the classroom blackboards. Any teacher foolish enough to leave sentences written across the board will find next day that all spelling mistakes have been circled in chalk. And any teacher guilty of more than one error is liable to find '8/10 – teacher must try harder' chalked alongside.

Our cleaner doesn't limit her attentions to blackboards. First-year junior teacher Mr Scott found his notice to parents, 'The sponsered [sic] walk is on Friday', circled in red felt-tip, and Mrs Haw's carefully written poster advertising the Summer Bazzar [sic] was awarded an exasperated underlining and several red felt-tip exclamation marks.

Our cleaner (who suspects that teachers are paid somewhat more than £1.8026 per hour) once grumbled to me about these modern standards.

'What you must appreciate,' I explained to her (as it had been explained to me when I once raised a similar query with the Head of English), 'is that today, lucid self-expression is considered to be more important in children's written work than the mechanics of spelling. It is felt that a child who has produced, for example, a page of flowing creative writing might lose heart if that page were to be returned to him peppered with spelling corrections.'

Our cleaner said that I seemed to have missed the point. She was talking about *teachers* being unable to spell correctly – not children.

It is not only in the classroom that attention to spelling has lapsed. Mistakes abound in newspapers, books and correspondence generally, and I have heard it argued that in an age when the written word is becoming less important than electronic audio and visual forms of communication, then so long as *some* people know how to spell correctly, it doesn't matter if most don't. ('What do you think I keep *you* for!' a headteacher once snapped at me when I jokingly pointed out the number of errors in the letter she had given me to copy type.)

This unconcerned attitude is reflected in many of the letters I see from teachers seeking employment, and it seems to be shared, moreover, by those who plan the interviews. It is my job to open the envelopes of all the applicants for a vacant post, and while a letter of copper-plate handwriting with a neatly-typed curriculum vitae may win *my* heart (for nothing is so infuriating than having to plough through a long badly written letter in order to try and find out whether 'J. Taylor' is Mr, Mrs, Miss or Ms) it won't necessarily impress the head or the school governors. I was once astonished when the writer of a hastily scrawled letter containing five spelling mistakes was shortlisted, and even more astonished when she got the job. (She came to interview wearing a skirt with a drooping hemline and with visible holes in her tights too; but that's another story.)

I have now had twelve years experience of reading letters of application from teachers and although I can rarely guess which ones will be called for interview I can usually pick out those who won't.

'Being the wife of a diplomat . . .' was the start of the opening sentence of a letter from one lady. She wished to impress us with the fact that she was

106

much-travelled and had taught children of many different races and colour. She might have been a tremendous asset to any primary school, but I knew she didn't even stand a chance of an interview at ours. Mr Masterton would have got no further than those first six words before slipping the letter onto the 'reject' pile.

Another lady who seemed to have a lot to offer (she was musical, artistic and athletic) wrote a calamitous last paragraph to an otherwise wholly acceptable letter:

> Since leaving Scotland I have not sought another teaching post until now because I have been extremely busy finishing my book 'With God's Help – A Study of Alternative Methods to assist the Difficult Child'. My previous published works are 'Singing along with Jesus' (a collection of simple international songs), 'Are you There?' (a collection of prayers for children) and 'We are Together' (short stories suitable for Primary School Assemblies).

'Ye Gods!' said Mr Masterton, slipping the letter on to the 'reject' pile. 'She'd certainly put the dampers on staffroom conversation.'

Applicants for teaching posts should remember that primary school heads are, usually, quite humble and ordinary people, and while they certainly wish to employ competent teachers they are also very concerned about staff relationships. Lucky is the head who has a team of reasonably happy teachers working with him/her, because exasperation, frustration, downright rows and hysterics won't be confined to the staffroom; it will all spill over into the head's office and the head has to sort it out.

So applicants who are middle-class, scholarly, intellectual, or with strong, unswerving convictions, either political, religious or sociological, must also be clever. Clever enough to conceal these drawbacks in their letters of application for teaching posts. It may also help to include one or two spelling mistakes.

Although the current casual attitude to the written word irritates me I have to accept that this is the way things are. But while *I* do my best to come to terms with these changing standards our school cleaner remains inflexibly critical. However, she told me last week that she will be leaving us at the end of the month which is, perhaps, just as well. She is going to work for the Health Service at our local hospital where, hopefully, her elementary school education won't be such an embarrassment (embarasment? . . . embbarasement?) and where, she tells me, she will earn a bit more than £1.8026 per hour.

17

Mr Masterton was taking a short cut across the waste ground beside the school (the garage that does his MOT tests is the other side), when his eye was caught by a yellow plastic lunchbox on the ground beside an elder bush. It was a clean-looking box, shaped like a small attaché case, with a handle on the top and a picture of Paddington Bear on the side. He guessed that it belonged to a child who attended Commercial Street School and he picked his way through the tussocky grass and rubble towards the bush.

Bending down to retrieve the box he noticed that beside it, and almost completely concealed by the branches brushing the ground, was a pair of sandals containing feet wearing clean white socks. He squatted down, pulled aside the branches, and saw that the lunch box and feet belonged to Lucy Baxter who was sitting with her knees drawn up to her chin and looking out at him with a frightened face down which the tears were pouring.

'Lucy,' said Mr Masterton, 'why are you sitting under this bush crying?'

Lucy was crying so much she found it difficult to reply. 'I (gasp), I (gulp), I don't feel very well.'

Mr Masterton managed to convince Lucy that sitting under a wet elder bush and surrounded by battered beer cans, bits of wood, old crisp packets and crumbling bricks wasn't going to make her feel any better and she agreed to come out and to be led across to school.

But she didn't stop crying. She was still crying when he brought her into the office and sat her upon my typing stool.

'I don't feel very well,' she sobbed, 'I want to go home.'

Lucy hadn't been at Commercial Street School very long but she was already well-known to me because she was always being sent to the office on account of her not feeling very well. Sometimes it was tummy ache; sometimes a headache, but usually she was 'feeling sick'. Her mother had long since lost patience.

'She's always perfectly all right when I get her home,' she said, 'I'm sure there's nothing *really* wrong with her.'

We came to the conclusion that Lucy was perhaps taking rather a long time to settle into her new school and that, hopefully, in time the tummy aches and sickness would go away.

Mr Masterton tore a couple of feet of toilet paper from my emergency roll, mopped up Lucy's face and persuaded her to blow her nose. By assuring her that of course she could go home if she wasn't well, he managed to persuade her to stop crying. And then he started to talk to her. He asked her how old she was; discovered that it was her birthday next week and then the talk went on to bicycles, kittens and a pet rabbit.

I interrupted him to tell him that the School Dentist was on the 'phone for him and that also the caretaker was waiting to see him, but he waved me away. Lucy talked happily about her rabbit, named Lucas, whom she fed every morning and cleaned out once a week on Saturdays.

Then Mr Masterton brought the subject around to school. Lucy was in a second-year junior class.

'What will you be doing this morning?' he asked.

Lucy reacted as though she had been slapped in the face. Her head dropped to her chest and she started crying again.

'Tables!' she yelped. 'We're doing the 9 times table and I don't know it.'

To-day was Thursday. Were the children in Lucy's class tested on their tables every Thursday? Was it always on a Thursday that Lucy was ill? I hadn't noticed.

'Is that all?' Mr Masterton grabbed a sheet of typing paper and drew up a chair to sit beside Lucy. 'But the 9 times table is easy . . . look, I'll show you. You know that two 9s are 18 don't you?'

Lucy nodded, but stared hopelessly at the sheet of paper upon which Mr Masterton had written the figure 18.

'Right, now to get three 9s all you have to do is to add one to the first number, and take away one from the second number. So 1 plus 1 equals 2, and 8 minus one equals 7. So three 9s are 27. Now, just do the same to get four 9s; add 1 to the 2 and take away 1 from the 7. So four 9s are 36. Get it?'

Lucy was looking a bit perkier. 'Now, you tell me what five 9s are.'

Lucy stared at the figure 36 thoughtfully. 'Forty-five?'

Mr Masterton gave her the pencil. 'Now, carry on and do the rest of the table.'

Lucy completed it without hesitation.

'I'll show you something else.' Mr Masterton took the pencil away from her. 'You're going to be the only child in the class who can do the 11 times table with very big numbers. If you want to multiply 11 by 23, for example, all you have to do is to move the 2 and the 3 apart so there's a space between them, then add 2 and 3 together (that makes 5) and insert that 5 between the 2 and the 3. So eleven 23s are 253. Now you write down what eleven 43s are.'

Lucy took the pencil and wrote down the figures 4 and 3 with a space between, then put a 7 in between. 'Is that right?' she said.

'Well, you do it the long way by making a sum out of it, and you'll see.'

She laboriously wrote down the figures, multi-plying 11 by 43 and came up with the same answer. She looked up at him and smiled.

'Off you go,' he said, 'and see if anyone else can do the 11 times table.'

Lucy trotted to the door.

'What are three 9s?' Mr Masterton called after her.

She hesitated for a moment; her eyes staring into space, her lips moving slightly. 'Twenty-seven!'

At playtime Lucy came running into the office. 'Miss gave me a star because I got the 9 times table right!'

'Don't let it go to your head,' said Mr Masterton. 'What are eleven 52s?'

Almost without pause came, 'Five hundred and seventy-two.'

'Four 9s,' he snapped.

A hesitation for half a minute, then the correct answer came.

'Five 9s,' he shouted, 'six 9s, seven 9s!'

Lucy was now giggling and snapping the answers straight back at him.

'Out you go to play now,' he said, and Lucy turned

to go. 'Eleven 61s!' he roared at her as she got to the door.

'Six hundred and seventy-one!' she shouted back, and danced off out into the playground.

'That,' said Mr Masterton, 'is what teaching is all about.'

Part IV
Suffer little children

18

Jenny is a happy chatterbox. Other children come to my office each morning with the class dinner register and just dump it onto my desk with a giggle and then scurry away. But six-year-old Jenny always stops to chat.

'Do you know what?' she always says.

'What?' I always reply.

And then Jenny goes on to tell me about the things that have happened at home – the aunties who have called – the children who have come to tea . . .

'And today I am going to Sharon's party and I'm wearing my best pink dress that Auntie Jean made and I've got a present all wrapped up in pretty paper and it's a secret, so I can't tell you.'

From Jenny's chatter I have learned all about the new car Daddy bought and the dolls' house he made her. When Jenny's baby brother was born the chatter reached a new peak of excitement.

' . . .And he's small and pink and has tiny little fingers, *much* tinier than mine and we're going to call him Sam.'

I received a daily report upon the progress of Sam. I heard how the christening went, how Auntie Jean made Sam some white booties, and how Sam was very good and didn't cry very much. Then, one afternoon, Jenny's mother – looking white and distraught – came early to collect her and I learned later from talk in the staffroom that baby Sam – healthy, bouncing, adored and cherished – had been found lying lifeless in his bedroom one morning; a victim of the mysterious 'cot death'.

Jenny was absent from school the following day, and when she re-appeared at the end of the week she was very pale and her eyes stared out from her face round and bewildered. She crept to my desk with the dinner register and looked up at me. 'My baby brother died,' she announced.

Jenny continued to come to school each day, and she carried out her normal duties with a thoughtful, puzzled and detached manner. Then, on the day of the funeral she was absent again. Mr Masterton wrote a letter to Jenny's parents; the school sent some flowers, and we all grieved for Jenny and her family.

Two days later Jenny was back at school.

'Do you know what?' she said, running into my office with the dinner register.

'What?' I replied.

'We said goodbye to Sam the day before yesterday, and there were lots and lots of flowers, and baby Sam was in a lovely little white box and he was covered with flowers and I wore my best white dress and my long white socks and new black shoes and I put a special bunch of flowers on the white box for Sam, and now he's gone to Jesus.'

I can only imagine what sort of terrible scar this tragedy must have left upon Jenny's mother, but to Jenny herself the life and death of Baby Sam is now being placed tidily away alongside all those other ups and downs of life that you have to cope with when you are six years old, and a happy chatterbox.

19

A child with something urgent to communicate will approach the nearest adult, and at Commercial Street School many of the children assume that all adults there are able to help them with their schooling. I once saw a child holding up his maths book to a baffled dinner lady. He wanted her to help with a problem. She didn't know what he was talking about and was obliged to tell him so. The boy was dumbfounded.

I could almost see the thoughts forming behind his eyes: if dinner ladies couldn't understand Nuffield Maths, then how could they expect *him* to work it out! And as the children are not totally confined to their classrooms, but carry out work in the library, the reading room and sometimes the playground, they assume that the office is just another work area – with me there to serve their purposes.

Children are sometimes sent with their exercise books to Mr Masterton – to show him what they have done. If Mr Masterton is not in his office they bring their books to me. Sometimes they are sent because the work they have done is very good and sometimes they are sent because it is very bad. It is not always easy for me to tell the difference. When in doubt I rely on the child's demeanour to guide me. Those who proffer their books eagerly and stand beaming expectantly up into my face have done some good work. Those with hanging heads and books half concealed behind them have not. But sometimes I make mistakes.

'Good heavens, is that all you've done this morning?' I once said sternly to a silent blank-faced boy who had handed me his book. With large ill-formed letters the words 'I wen to a purty las nit' had been pencilled across the top half of an otherwise blank page. I learned later that never before at this school had this child been persuaded to put pencil to paper and those seven words were the first he had written. I am now a little more circumspect.

'I think you had better bring this back later and show Mr Masterton,' I say, in a not-too-bright, but not-too-stern voice – and (hopefully) the children will interpret this to suit the circumstances.

'Please can we measure your head?' a child once said, running into the office. She held the tape measure whilst her colleague carried the clipboard, paper and pencil. 'It's for our maths.'

I have also been questioned on what I remember about the last war, what I have for breakfast, and been asked to complete a questionnaire about my favourite drinks. Usually I co-operate with these tasks in a mildly resigned manner, but sometimes I am cross.

'Go away; I'm too busy,' I said to the bevy of juniors who came complete with tape recorder to 'do' an interview for their class newspaper. I wish I had said the same to the children who wanted to 'draw round' me. This involved going out into the hall and lying spreadeagled upon a very large piece of white cardboard while the children crawled around me with a black crayon.

It is possible that anyone connected with the primary school education system may not be surprised to find the school secretary lying prone in the entrance hall, but the man who came that morning to collect for the RSPCA thought he had an emergency on his hands.

I didn't mind running three times around the playground while the children timed me with a stop watch – particularly when I discovered that only the most athletic boy in the school had made a faster time (whereas Mr Masterton had given up after one lap) – but all this entering-into-the-spirit-of-the-thing sometimes takes large chunks out of my working day.

I tried to explain this to the LEA's accountant when he dropped in for an unexpected check a few weeks back. He made very stern remarks about the state of our dinner books, he found that I was 23p over in the petty cash, and he complained that we were holding far too much money in the school.

'But I can never find time to go to the bank,' I explained.

On the same day Miss Baker had asked me if I had yet

118

found time to type out the infant song sheets, and Mr Masterton was muttering that it was about time that we sent out the camp letters.

'I really must keep the children out of this office and get down to some work,' I grumbled to myself, pushing the door shut. And then there was a tap on the door and in came Melinda, Ruth and Amelia.

'Can we play you our new piece? We've been practising it all week.'

Melinda arranged herself behind her trombone, Ruth put her lips to her bass recorder, and Amelia stood in front of them holding a sheet of music paper covered with a lot of pencilled notes. They blew away lustily and quite tunefully for a few minutes. There were a few notes that sounded a bit like *Pictures from an Exhibition*, but also a bit of *Swan Lake* seemed to creep in.

'Very nice,' I said when they had finished. 'I didn't recognise it; what was it?'

'We made it up,' said Amelia. 'We've called it "Jungle Moonlight".'

I can win back some time, to a certain extent, by seeking help from the children with routine work in the office. When the Summer Fair programmes have to be folded and numbered, the Swimming Gala or Sports Day lists sorted and stapled together, or four hundred circulars counted out, folded and put into envelopes, I ask one of the fourth-year teachers if I can borrow a couple of children with clean hands.

Any excuse to get out of the classroom is seized upon with delight by the children and 'helping Mrs West' is a much coveted and argued-about opportunity. They come charging across the playground whooping with enthusiasm. If I am lucky it will be two girls – I *always* request girls – but some teachers (more concerned with sexual equality than with providing me with the most efficient workers) will sometimes send me boys. Anyone who has tried to employ lively ten-year-old boys on routine and repetitive tasks will know why I prefer girls.

Counting the photograph money is a good example. Following the visit of the school photographer, parents who wish to buy photographs will send money into the school office in the little brown envelopes which the photographer has provided. I can be faced with the task of opening up and checking six hundred or so envelopes and am grateful for any help I can get.

I sit the children on the floor with the wastepaper bin in front of them and some empty large ice-cream tubs between them. I ask them to open the envelopes; check that the contents agree with the amount written on the front, then divide the money between the ice-cream boxes – putting, say, cheques and notes in one box, and sorting coins into the others. Then, if they have time, they can count the money into bank bags, which I will provide.

Little girls will work steadily through the envelopes (gossiping quietly all the while, but still remembering to read the front of each one), then they will divide the final task between themselves ('I'll do the cheques and notes, and you do the coins') and when they have finished they will hover at my desk, asking if there is anything else to do. Of course I have to check the money again, but I usually find that little girls make few mistakes; moreover the notes will be neatly stacked, all facing the same way and held together with a paper clip.

Little boys will start the job eagerly enough, but they will argue about methods of working ('No, stupid, put the coins all in piles of ten first of all – then fill the bags all in one go!'). And they will compete with each other for speed ('I've done six bags and all these cheques whilst you've only done four bags of 2ps'). They will swap places before long ('I'm fed up with doing all these cheques – you do some and let me count the pound coins'), then they will both get bored and finish the job in a rush, then ask if they can go. Later I will find mistakes in most of the bags, notes in a haphazard muddle, some pound coins underneath my desk and a few cheques inside envelopes that were thrown away.

I think I have touched on a fundamental fact of life here. Anthropological books describing family life among primitive tribes sometimes comment (least-ways they have done so in the few that I have read) on the fact that the women and female children do most of the work whilst the men laze in the sun and the boys lark about on the river bank chucking stones into the water.

The implication is that we in civilised parts treat our womenfolk better. But I think that the primitive tribes have got it right. I am sure that little girls *want* to help their mothers shift the earth and gather the harvest, and they are perfectly competent to do so. Little boys are not capable of doing anything else *but* lie on the river bank chucking stones into the water.

Helpful mums who come in to take cookery classes generally prefer to have more girls than boys in a group. They too find that girls will listen to and follow instructions, whereas boys will argue and mess about. And although we have plenty of naughty girls in the school the cookery mums tell me that the child who throws pastry at the wall (to see if it will stick) or shoves a finger into every egg on the tray (to see how much pressure it takes to break one) or writes its name in loops of golden syrup across the table, will always be a *boy*.

And certainly, when it comes to presenting samples of their work to me in the office, the girls will be more polite than the boys. A girl will bring a plateful of scones or flapjacks and hold it out, inviting me to take one. A boy will run in with his plate, lift off a piece of cooked dough, dump it on my desk saying, 'That's your piece,' and run out again.

This brings me to a rather delicate problem. Before the cookery class starts the children will have been supervised whilst they washed their hands. Hygiene in the cookery room is considered to be extremely important, but the helpful mum, moving busily between stove, sink and the table where the children are working their dough or stirring their cake mixture, may not notice the little nose about to drip, those little fingers investigating places that they shouldn't, that tousled little head scattering hair and maybe head lice.

All this goes through my mind when a smiling child enters the office carrying a plate of cookery-class delicacies.

'They look absolutely delicious,' I say, selecting a piece and putting it upon my shorthand pad. 'I'll keep it to have later with my coffee.'

As soon as the child has left the office I throw the cake into my wastepaper bin – making sure that it is well hidden. Occasionally I am nearly caught out.

'But I want you to eat it *now*,' said one persistent little boy. 'I want you to say what it tastes like.' He was very proud of the gingerbread man he had made. 'That's real currants there,' he said, prodding the doughy biscuit with a rather grubby forefinger. 'That's his eyes, and that's the buttons down his front.'

'I shall really look forward to having it with my coffee,' I said. 'I mustn't stop now. I must finish typing this letter for Mr Masterton.'

'When are you going to have your coffee?'

'In about fifteen minutes' time.'

I heard him scamper off down the corridor, but I had barely managed to conceal the gingerbread man in my bin before he was back again.

'Is it time for your coffee yet?' He came across and looked around the desk. 'Where's my gingerbread man?'

122

'Well, he looked so tempting I couldn't wait for my coffee, and he was delicious,' I said in a gabble. 'Now off you go.'

He paused at the door. 'You *sure* you ate it?'

'It was scrumptious!' I said, looking at my type-writer.

Mr Masterton has no such cowardly qualms. Any child bringing him a plate of cakes will stand by and watch him take one, eat it, and say how good it is. A little girl running in one day with her plate of butter-fly cream cakes tripped over her shoelace and went sprawling. The plate flew out of her hand and the cakes rolled under my table.

We all scrabbled about on the floor picking them up and Mr Masterton and I tried to reassure her that it didn't matter a bit that some of the tops had fallen off.

'But they're all squiffy now,' she said, close to tears, 'and there's bits of dirt in the cream.'

She blew energetically over the cakes in an attempt to shift some of the dirt and prodded the bits of broken top on each cake in order to straighten them up.

Mr Masterton took one of the cakes, carefully removed a few hairs, and bit into it. 'Lovely,' he said, 'I think being squiffy improves them – and makes it easier to bite.'

I took a particularly battered one and put it on my shorthand pad. 'I shall really enjoy having this with my coffee later on.'

I have seen Mr Masterton falter only once when sampling children's cookery. This was when the first-year juniors were doing a project on How the Romans Lived and it was decided to experiment with a few Roman dishes during the cookery lesson.

Now 'Roman toast' I can thoroughly recommend. It appeared to be small squares of fried bread with runny honey poured all over it. I was quite happy to sample some because on this particular occasion the helpful mum had fried the bread at home and then poured the honey over it in the classroom whilst the children watched.

But 'Roman soup' – a concoction of pennyroyal, pearl barley and fishbones – did not appeal. The children had started cooking it the day before. A great vat of the stuff had been steaming malevolently in the school kitchen all the previous afternoon and Cook said that the smell of it kept reminding her that it was time she cleaned out the 'fridge.

A few more hours of cooking and the Roman soup was ready to be shared out. It was ladled out into small plastic cups, then three little girls dressed in their Roman costumes and carrying trays full, came smiling into the office.

'Thank you dear,' I said, taking a cup. 'I shall enjoy having that later on with my coffee.' It was dark grey with even darker grey and brown bits floating on top.

Mr Masterton took a cup and stared at it. He then looked at me. I smiled. He looked back at the little girls. They smiled. He lifted the cup to his lips and took a sip.

For a while the pennyroyal, pearl barley and fish-bone fluid remained in his mouth. A few beads of sweat broke out upon his brow. Then, with a gulp, he swallowed.

'Delicious,' he gasped – and hastily left the room.

20

The man standing beside my desk was tall and thin. He had prominent cheekbones, cold-looking eyes behind thick glasses and a mouth like a straight pencilled line. I sensed trouble.

'What do I have to do,' the man said, 'to ensure that my child is not given meat to eat at lunchtime?'

I could not recall having seen the man before so I explained, as I do to all parents whose children ask for vegetarian meals, that the kitchen is perfectly happy to provide them but we do not wish to be at the mercy of passing childish fads so we require a letter from the parent making the request.

'I have done that,' the man said, 'I did that when my boy started here last term. I have also been personally to see your Cook. So I repeat my question. What do I have to do to ensure that my child is not given meat to eat at lunchtime?'

'Provide him with a packed lunch,' I snapped, and then regretted it. If something had gone wrong with our system I wasn't going to improve matters by making sarcastic remarks. 'I cannot understand why your child has been given meat. I will look into it and make sure that it doesn't happen again.'

When I discussed it later with Cook she was very puzzled, but realised what had happened when she consulted her list of names.

'Oh, little *Roland*! — Yes, I remember his Dad coming in . . . but these last few weeks Roland has been *asking* for meat; he *likes* meat, so I assumed he was no longer vegetarian and I crossed him off my list. But I'll make sure he goes back on it.'

The next morning Roland's father came to the office again. 'Is it of the slightest use me telling you that Roland was, once again, given meat to eat yesterday; or do I have to go and speak to somebody else about this?'

I decided, in defence of the school cook, that Roland's father must be told the facts about Roland's appetite.

'In a very busy kitchen, with several kitchen staff serving the children, it is very difficult to ensure that a child receives a vegetarian meal when that child actually asks for meat.'

'What!' The word came out like a whiplash.

I was beginning to feel a little fearful for Roland, but I couldn't change course now.

'Roland enjoys meat dishes, and he *asks* for them,' I repeated.

'Oh he does, does he?' Roland's father turned a frosty face towards my window and stared across the playground. He was obviously thinking nasty thoughts. He then said slowly, 'We shall have to see about that,' and he walked out of the office.

'Why on earth did you give him meat again?' I asked Cook next time I saw her.

She looked a little guilty. 'Well, it was sausages yesterday,' she said, 'and I told Roland he wasn't supposed to eat meat and he agreed that this was so but said that sausages were all right – he was allowed them. Anyway . . . poor little lad; he's only four, and he does love his dinners so much.'

'Well, he mustn't have meat again. He's going to be in trouble when he gets home today because of those sausages.'

A few days later, at the start of the infants' dinner break, a child came running to the office.

'Cook says could you please come to the kitchen immediately.'

They were waiting for me when I got to the kitchen. The serving-up had come to a halt. Cook stood there with a plate of salad in one hand. It was an attractive plate of salad, with lettuce, tomato, celery, a hard-boiled egg and grated cheese, but she waved a tablespoon at the child heading the queue at her counter.

'I'm trying to make him take this salad but he's refusing. Says he wants steak and kidney pie.'

Roland was so small that he could see over the counter only by standing on tiptoe and catching hold of the edge. One little hand clutched his knife, fork and spoon. The steak and kidney pie had just been cut and pieces of beef, kidney and mushrooms spilled out from beneath a golden crust – crisp on top but soft and moist inside. A rich brown gravy was just beginning to flow. The pie was about six inches away from Roland's nose and the steam from it was clouding his glasses.

I wanted him to have the pie. I wanted him to have the pie – with carrots, peas and roast potatoes, and to have any second helpings that were going. But I thought of Roland's Dad. I thought of Roland standing at his Dad's knee this evening – those great bony hands trapping the boy's skinny arms . . .

'Now tell me, exactly *what* did you have to eat at school today.'

'Roland,' I said, 'take this lovely salad and go and sit down.' One day, perhaps, Roland will take his revenge.

That particular morning was quite a traumatic one in the infants' dining hall. A dinner lady who supervises the packed-lunch eaters went, with tears in her eyes, to see Cook. She was holding a small plastic sandwich box which she shook under Cook's nose.

'Just look what this child's been given for lunch today!' The box contained three small pieces of cold cooked potato, blackening slightly at the edges, and a half-eaten rissole – dried and hard, with congealed fat on top.

The lunchbox belonged to a five-year-old child (doomed to go through school life with the name of Flower Baggs) who was, in fact, entitled to free meals but whose mother every so often insisted on the child bringing food from home because she considered that school dinners were too starchy and that this was the reason Flower had occasional 'violent outbursts of temper'.

I had never noticed any outbursts of temper from Flower who was a quiet, rather pathetic creature in school, but Mrs Baggs and her strange notions were well known to all of us. Her two other children

(Jewell Baggs and Dagger Baggs) had now left us for secondary school, but during their time with us they too had been obliged to eat some strange things from home.

The reason for the dinner lady's concern on this particular occasion was that she had found Flower staring hopelessly into her lunchbox, quite obviously unable to make herself eat any of its contents. When questioned, Flower said that this was the remains of last night's evening meal and her mother had said she was getting nothing else to eat until she had finished it all up. Flower had refused to eat it at breakfast-time, and so she had eaten no food at all since the previous day.

Cook angrily emptied the contents of Flower's lunchbox into the school waste bin and served up a steak and kidney dinner for her. She then wondered whether she had done the right thing in throwing away the deteriorating remnants of Flower's dinner from home. Would her mother, believing that the child had eventually eaten the mess, be tempted to do this again? On the other hand, if the dinner remains had been taken back home again, how many other mealtimes would Flower have to sit looking at it?

During the same lunchtime, when I passed the infants' dinner queue I noticed Faith – who was crying. Now this was unusual. In spite of having a rather insecure and troubled family background (Faith's mother is a heroin addict), Faith is normally a happy, skippy little girl who seems to enjoy life.

'Faith! What's the matter?' I asked.

'I don't know,' she howled.

She was clutching her arms around her middle and I thought she had a tummy ache – but she said that she did not have a tummy ache; neither did she feel sick, nor was she in any pain at all.

'Then why are you crying?'

'I don't know,' she sobbed, 'I don't know.'

128

Later, when I went through the hall again I saw that Faith appeared to have forgotten whatever it was had been troubling her. She was tucking into her steak and kidney pie and was occasionally chatting to the person sitting opposite. After the infant lunch sitting I was in the playground and, bending down to retrieve a toy lorry stuck in a grating, I felt a slight tapping on my backside. Faith was there beaming up at me.

'I now know why I was crying,' she giggled, 'it was because I was so hungry!'

21

I was sitting in the staffroom eating my sandwiches and gazing absentmindedly out of the window overlooking the playground when I saw an astonishing thing. Ten-year-old Jonathan Starr was sprawled on the ground, propped up on one elbow and completely absorbed in a comic when seven-year-old Rhona Wilbert strolled past. As she drew level with him Rhona pulled up her dress, pulled down her knickers and thrust her bare bottom into Jonathan's face.

Jonathan, obviously startled, sat bolt upright, shuffled quickly backwards and then gathered up his comic and scurried away. Rhona yanked up her knickers again and skipped off — presumably in search of someone else a bit more co-operative. The whole incident was over in about thirty seconds.

Having finished choking on my beetroot sandwich I related what I had just seen, and Miss Baker quickly looked outside the staffroom door, grabbed the first child she saw and said, 'Go and find Rhona Wilbert and tell her to come here.'

A little while later there was a tap on the staffroom door and Miss Baker went outside to question Rhona. The conversation went something like this.

'Why did you pull your knickers down in the playground?'

'I didn't.'

'But Rhona, you have just been seen pulling down your knickers.'

'I didn't . . . it was Johnny Starr. I only walked past him and he put his hand up my skirt and pulled down my knickers . . .'

Which only goes to show that some females become dangerous at a very early age.

I have noticed that children differ amazingly in their sexual awareness. Some seem to know what it is all about from infancy, and such children are not confined to the liberal 'let-it-all-hang-out' households. In our fourth-year junior class are two very talented young writers.

Julia, who is interested in history and architecture, writes well-researched and carefully thought-out pieces all about local Georgian houses and Norman churches. (I have ear-marked her for Faber & Faber) whereas Elspeth, who is interested in boys and disco-théques, covers page after page with passionate stories telling of dresses being ripped off, girls being thrown on to beds and car chases at midnight (Mills and Boon take note!). Both Julia and Elspeth have parents who are university lecturers.

In the same fourth-year class there is quiet little Amy Hambleton; not particularly talented, not particularly anything. But Mr and Mrs Hambleton (Plymouth Brethren) would have been horrified to read Amy's account of 'What we did at Camp': 'We were near the boys tents. One day the flap was back and Ben was taking his pants off and I saw his you-know-what. It was scrumptious!'

To a certain extent the girls' physical development and dress sense seems to match their sexuality. Julia is thin, flat-chested and always wears the school uniform, whereas Elspeth, with pouting breasts and rounded bottom, wiggles about the playground in well-cut fashionable skirts and blouses. But the blank-faced inscrutable Amy wears children's sandals and ankle socks.

I was a bit taken aback by a playground clapping chant I heard recently:

Ha, Ha, Ha,
Lost my bra,
Left my knickers in my boy-friend's car . . .

but then remembered that as a thirteen-year-old I giggled over a skipping rhyme:

Ask no questions, tell no lies,
I saw a Chinaman doing up his flies . . .

which seems to suggest that there has always been rudery in the playground. That the innuendo is ruder in the 1980s than it was in the 1940s is only to be expected.

For every sexually provocative little girl there will always be a following of little boys — all eager and willing to be provoked. Mostly they just want to look, whisper and snigger but one or two want to do a lot more. Nine-year-old Seth Hunter is one of these. Seth Hunter, a thin-faced rabbitty little boy with protruding teeth, has been a non-stop nuisance during the five years he has been attending Commercial Street School. He has been a nuisance to the class teachers unfortunate to have his name on their registers, a nuisance to the caretaker and a nuisance to the local residents unfortunate enough to live along the route Seth follows to school.

If bicycles are stolen, sheds broken into, trees uprooted, desks rifled, toilet rolls pushed down lavatory pans or gang fights organised, Seth Hunter will be involved — either as the organiser or as a whole-hearted participant.

But we were not aware of his sexual appetite until he was in the third-year junior class and one day wrote a note to Annette, a pink-faced innocent little girl with long blonde hair who sat the other side of the room. Mrs Cornell, the class teacher, noticed the slip of paper passing from hand to hand across the room and she intercepted it. She read it and was shocked. She sealed the note in an envelope and immediately dispatched it, in the hands of a reliable child, to Mr Masterton.

I was not permitted to see what it was that Seth wrote to Annette, but I gather from Mr Masterton's comments that Seth was suggesting things he would like to do to Annette and in return things he would like Annette to do to him. In all his years as a schoolteacher Mr Masterton had never, it seemed, seen such a disgusting note written by a child. 'I hadn't even *heard* of such practices until I went into the Army,' he said, 'and *then* I didn't believe it!'

After a lot of careful thought Mr Masterton decided what to do about the note. The one thing he would *not* do was to inform Seth's parents. Seth's mother (a thin-faced rabbitty little woman with protruding teeth) was mentally unstable. She sometimes roamed the streets muttering to herself and she was occasionally taken away to spend a few weeks as a voluntary patient at an appropriate institution.

When this happened various aunties were called upon to keep an eye on the family because Seth's dad, a long-distance/continental lorry driver, was away from home for much of the time. Letters of complaint about Seth's behaviour had in the past gone from school to home but had not had much effect until the day when one such letter coincided with a period when Seth's dad happened to be at home.

He came along to the school – a huge hunk of a man with thinning tight-curled blonde hair over a large red face – and he sat in Mr Masterton's office beside an obviously frightened Seth whilst the boy's latest misdeeds were related. When Mr Masterton told of the pieces of masonry Seth had been throwing through the open school kitchen window (some of which landed among the prepared salad dishes) Mr Hunter lifted one large red hand and clouted Seth across the face with such force that the boy fell from his chair.

Taken aback, Mr Masterton went on, somewhat hesitantly, to tell of a more serious incident when Seth kicked a dinner lady and used obscene language to her. With a growl of anger Mr Hunter stood up, grabbed Seth by the arm and flung him across the room. The boy's head thudded against the filing cabinet and he collapsed in a crumpled heap on the floor. Now thoroughly alarmed, Mr Masterton spent the next twenty minutes trying to calm Mr Hunter and he felt obliged to keep talking soothingly until he felt that both man and son were in a fit state to leave the office together. He didn't want another interview like that!

However, now knowing Seth's fear of his father, Mr Masterton saw no reason why the note should not be used as a weapon of blackmail in order to try and ensure some better behaviour from Seth during his remaining year at Commercial Street School. The boy was sent for, the note waved and the threat made.

To a certain extent this ploy has worked. For many weeks after the note-passing incident Seth was not involved in any episodes of bad behaviour. There was one slight lapse when Seth threw a hymn book across the room just before Assembly and was sent to stand outside the Hall. But when Mr Masterton spoke to him afterwards and said, somewhat thoughtfully, 'Now let me see, when is your father next home?' Seth immediately burst into tears and apologised and promised never to do it again.

But sex, I fear, will be the boy's undoing. A few

days ago, during dinnertime play, he was discovered behind the huts with a girl – apparently putting a few of his ideas into practice. Fortunately, a dinner lady appeared before things had developed very far and she led him crying and protesting loudly to Mr Masterton.

'I didn't do it!' Seth screeched. 'I didn't, I didn't, I didn't do it!'

Mr Masterton, who had just returned from the bank and who, rather wearily, had been hoping for a trouble-free lunch break, asked Seth to explain what it was that he hadn't done.

'I didn't put my hand on her fanny, nor I didn't bite her bum neither!'

But I don't believe him. The girl behind the huts with Seth was Rhona Wilbert – and we all know what *she* gets up to during playtimes.

22

Purity came to us at the age of four and a half years and with a reputation which made Mrs Snow (Reception class teacher) realise that the three terms ahead were going to be very difficult ones. Purity's parents (one of them black, the other white) had featured in her life for the first 3½ years only. During these 3½ years Purity had been thrashed with a studded belt, kicked in the back, starved and left lying alone for days at a time in a locked, unheated room.

Several months in hospital had repaired most of the physical damage to Purity, but her battered mind had not responded to treatment. A place had been found for her in a children's home but after six weeks it was decided that a children's home was not a suitable establishment for Purity and that she should be cared for in a one-to-one relationship. She was (said the children's home matron) a little animal.

A caring and well-intentioned foster mother was found, but after one week the good lady was asking to be relieved of the responsibility. She could not 'get through' to the child. A succession of foster mothers followed but none kept her for longer than a fortnight until Purity came to live with Mrs Temple.

Mrs Temple, who keeps an establishment for unwanted dogs, told me that she treated Purity in the same way and with the same patient but firm loving kindness that she gave to any other battered little stray that was brought to her. Purity responded by learning how to sit and eat at table, and by agreeing to sit upon a lap and be cuddled. She also learned that to put her hand into someone else's was a comfortable thing to do. But now she was old enough to attend school. Mrs Temple took Purity to the nearest school, explained the circumstances to the headmistress and registered the child for admission.

Three days later the headmistress was asking Mrs Temple to take her away again. Purity, the headmistress claimed, was not ready for a normal state education. She recommended that Mrs Temple apply for a place for the child at a residential school for educationally subnormal children. Mrs Temple disagreed. Mrs Temple felt that at the back of Purity's dark little mind there was a normal, intelligent little girl waiting to be released. So she brought her to us – the next nearest school.

It was agreed that for the first week Mrs Temple would bring Purity to school and stay with her in the classroom for half a morning, and then take her away again. Purity sat on Mrs Temple's lap in the corner and watched what was going on. But when anyone approached her she shrank back against Mrs Temple and when a small boy came up and offered her a toy car she lashed out and hit the car from his hand. She agreed to have a bottle of milk each day and as the week went by she seemed to relax. During the last two mornings she sat upon Mrs Snow's lap for a while and played with a puzzle. The time had come for her schooling to begin.

During the term that followed Mrs Snow gained the respect and unreserved admiration of all the staff, and the extreme gratitude of Mrs Temple. Purity, and society at large, will never know the debt owed to Mrs Snow. Lesser women than her would have given up or would have suffered a nervous breakdown. Mrs Snow gritted her teeth, probably gained a few more grey hairs, and carried on.

At first Purity refused to join in with any group activity, so she was sometimes left to play by herself in the book corner, in the hope that curiosity might encourage her to join in. One day she approached a table where four children were building with Play-People and Lego. Purity stood looking for a while and then reached over, grabbed several pieces, and ran away. Any attempt to try and persuade her to do something was met with violent temper. She deliberately tore up books, threw paint pots across the room, kicked, scratched and spat at the other children.

Purity rarely spoke, and she seemed to know only two words. During her first 3½ years of life no-one had spoken to her very much. And now, at 4½ years old, she could repeat only those words she had heard so many times before. A conversation with Purity went something like this:

'Hello, Purity, there's a pretty dress you're wearing to-day.'

*'Piss off.'

'Now run along and put your lunchbox on the table with the other ones.'

'Piss off.'

---

* This is not the four-letter word that Purity always used. Anyone who has shared a bus queue with a group of home-going school-children knows that four-letter obscenities form part of their every-day language. But in this book I prefer to use a less offensive expletive.

'Would you like to put these pieces of puzzle together, Purity?'

'Piss off.'

Occasionally, when Purity seemed to be beside herself with rage, Mrs Snow would send for help. She would dispatch a child to Mr Masterton with a piece of paper with the letters 'S.O.S.' written on it. Mr Masterton would abandon whatever it was he had been doing and would go at once to the reception classroom. He would pick up Purity and carry her down to the office. She screamed, she kicked, she punched his chest, she pulled his tie, she tried to scratch his face, she spat at him.

He sat in my office and held Purity firmly on his lap, saying stern but gentle things, like 'Now come on Purity, this is very naughty, you mustn't do this,' while Purity carried on scratching, screeching, kicking his knees and lashing out around her. He would sit there holding her until, exhausted, she would go limp and cry, sobbing into his chest. He then cuddled her for a while and then carried her back to Mrs Snow. And so it went on, week in, week out.

We began to get complaints from other parents. 'That little coloured girl – she kicked our Terry so hard the other day he's still got the bruise; and she bit him last week too. It's never right; there's special schools for creatures like her . . . she shouldn't be in with normal children.'

But Mrs Snow and Mr Masterton persisted and gradually, very gradually, Purity began to respond. It was story-reading time that first captured her interest. When the story is read the children all sit on the floor in the book corner, and Mrs Snow noticed that when she got out the book to read the day's story Purity was always the first child to scrabble across to the corner to sit on the carpet.

It was during the reading of a story that Mrs Snow

first saw Purity smile, and on another occasion she saw her laugh and clap her hands. Thereafter, when she saw that Purity was about to have a tantrum she gathered her up, sat the child on her lap, and read her a story. When Purity's mind had calmed down with the story Mrs Snow would then try to discuss with her the problem that had threatened the tantrum. Somehow, in between dealing with Purity, Mrs Snow managed to teach the rest of the class as well.

By the end of the year Purity was ready, with the rest of her classmates, to move up into Miss Allen's class. Within the secure framework of home life with Mrs Temple and school life with Mrs Snow Purity had learned that life could be happy and that it was more comfortable if you followed certain rules. She went, when told, to wash her hands and line up for dinner. She stood still in the playground when the whistle went after play, and she walked back to her classroom quietly with the other children.

We were worried that the change when moving up to Miss Allen's class might unsettle her but, after a cautious first week, Purity found that Miss Allen was kind and gentle just like Mrs Snow and the child accepted the slightly different daily routine without difficulty.

One day I saw Purity in the playground. She was involved with several other little girls in a clapping, chanting game and she was laughing. The game came to an end, the children drifted apart and Purity started skipping about. Aimlessly, and for no other reason than that she was a happy little girl playing in the sunshine, Purity skipped round and round the playground, little coffee-coloured knees bobbing up and down. Then she saw me. She waved and ran across.

'Hello Mrs West!'

I knew then that we were winning with Purity.

But it is a very fragile victory. Purity can cope with

life only if events happen around her as she thinks they should. If she finds another child's coat on her peg; if someone takes her pencil away; if she loses her lunchbox or if the task set for her is something she doesn't want to do, Purity is liable at any time to lose her temper and kick or punch the person nearest to her.

Last week we had a visit from the LEA's Senior Adviser for Arts. He is a very important man and as Commercial Street School has a reputation for imaginative and creative art work, we were determined that the school would be looking as attractive as possible, with artistic displays on all walls of the corridors, and each class working on its current art project.

Now Purity thoroughly enjoys painting and she is showing considerable promise. For the occasion of the Senior Adviser's visit Purity was painting a tiger. It was a very good tiger. It covered the entire piece of paper and Miss Allen said that it was the best tiger she had seen. It just so happened that Purity's tiger was black – all black, and it had a squarish sort of face with two pointed ears on top.

The Senior Adviser stopped by Purity's desk and admired her work.

'There's a lovely doggie!' he said.

The smile faded from Purity's face.

'It really is a beautiful doggie,' he went on, and he picked up Purity's painting and held it up to the rest of the class. 'Look what a lovely doggie this little girl has painted.'

Purity's head drooped and she stared at the top of her table. She was scowling and angry.

The Senior Adviser replaced the painting on her table and bent over her. 'I think we ought to give your doggie a name,' he said beaming. 'What shall we call him?'

'Piss off,' said Purity.

23

The old lady who lives in a top-floor flat in the house next door to the school once told me that she hated the school holidays because then the premises of Commercial Street School were just a dead and dreary collection of stained and crumbling buildings.

'During term time the place is alive with children, and I love to watch them from my window.'

The old lady regulated her day by the school bells, which she could hear quite plainly, and she made sure that during playtimes and dinner times she was sitting in her window overlooking the playground while she drank her coffee or ate her lunch. Seeing the children at play, she said, reminded her of her own childhood. I can understand this.

The yells, squeals and laughter from a playground in the 1980s must sound exactly the same as those which came from a children's playground in the early 1900s. And some of the chanting and clapping games are *exactly* the same. 'The Farmer's in his Den' has been around for a few generations, and so has 'The Good Ship Sails through the Alley Alley Ooh.' Why is it, I wonder, that some chanting games last down the centuries (like 'Oranges and Lemons'), whereas others disappear after a short while?

When I was a junior we used to do fast skipping to a rhyme 'Archi-ball, ball, ball, King of the Jew, Jew, Jews, bought his wife, wife, wife, a pair of shoe, shoe, shoes,' but I never hear this now. Come to think of it, I never see fast-skipping now. Don't the girls do 'bumps' any more? (This is where the rope passes twice beneath your feet during the course of one jump.)

The long skipping rope with several children jumping is still in fashion – 'All in together, this fine weather' – and they also do a new-fangled slow-moving thing with long pieces of elastic tape which I am told is 'French skipping'. Yes, I can quite understand the old lady's delight in watching the children at play, and if I could take my coffee up there and join her I could share her delight. But I can't. I have to sit here in the office during playtime, waiting for all the injuries to come in.

Children who rush around playgrounds with ropes, balls, conkers on bits of string and with arms flailing will injure themselves. They always have done. But a potentially lethal hazard that the old lady would not have seen in *her* childhood playground is the climbing frame. Anyone who thinks that climbing frames are good things to have in children's playgrounds should come and spend a few playtimes sitting in my office and help me make the right decisions about the fractured skulls, broken kneecaps, splintered jawbones and cases of concussion that are carried in.

I think the jawbones are the worst. A child swinging on the top rung of a frame may let go and on the way down to the ground catch its chin on the lower bars. As well as the cracked jaw-bone there may be a few broken teeth and a tongue bitten through. Under these circumstances first-aid is limited to comfort, consolation and the immediate summoning of an ambulance. In less dramatic accidents I will try to contact parents first, but if there is likely to be a delay, Mr Masterton will take the child to hospital.

The seriousness of an accident cannot always be judged by a child's reaction. A little girl once came to the office to say that she had fallen down and hurt her arm. There was no visible injury and she seemed to be able to move her arm without very much difficulty, so I just sat her down and told her to wait a while 'to see how it goes'.

Her friend stayed with her and they chatted away happily until, after about five minutes, the girl said she felt better now and asked if they could go out again. Later that evening the girl told her mother about the accident and said that the arm still hurt. She was taken to hospital where an X-ray revealed that the arm was broken in two places. On another occasion a little girl was carried in screaming with pain, saying she had hurt her back and couldn't move. We called an ambulance. She was still screaming when the ambulance men carried her out. But there was absolutely nothing wrong with her. She was back with us in the afternoon, skipping about the playground as usual.

When a child is injured and in pain my first concern is to do the right thing for that child. My second concern is to make sure that we can *prove* that the school has done the right thing for the child. Angry parents threatening litigation are feared by head-teachers who haven't 'covered' themselves. The LEA demands that we complete and submit forms to them detailing all serious accidents to children.

In addition to this Mr Masterton insists that we keep a 'Bump Book' into which is written an account of every accident on the school premises. Although writing up these incidents is a nuisance (the task usually falls to me) the Bump Book has come in useful.

'These headaches that Sebastian keeps having are now affecting his vision,' a mother once said to me. 'The Doctor suggested that they could have started with a bang on the head. Sebastian tells me that he had a bad accident in the playground about a year ago and *nothing was done about it.*'

I asked Sebastian to describe the accident and he said that he had collided with Joe and their heads crashed together. With mother standing beside the desk I got out the Bump Book and flipped back through the pages. I found the entry.

10th Sept. Sebastian Tucker collided with Joseph Barnett during morning play. No visible injury on either boy. Sebastian felt a little dizzy so sat in office.

Later said he felt better and asked to go out to play.
Mother informed by telephone.

I don't know what value my scribbled entry would
have been in a court of law – but it certainly took the
wind out of mother's sails.

'Oh yes . . . I'd forgotten that,' she said.

Teachers on duty in the playground when an accident happens usually write an account in the Bump
Book. Playground ladies try to avoid doing the job.
They are on duty at dinner times and sometimes I
return from lunch to find scribbled little notes on my
shorthand pad: 'Sam, Miss Baker's class. Bang on
nose.' 'Brick fell on head out of tree. Little ginger haired
boy.'

If the playground ladies know I am in the office they
will send the children to me – but even then it sometimes takes a long time to get the facts. A junior child
once brought to the office a tiny infant.

'Mrs Stubbs says this little girl bumped her head and
will you put it in the Book, please.'

'What's your name?' I asked the infant.

'Trays,' she whispered.

Now even with four hundred children on roll I think
I would have remembered if we had a child with the
name of Trays in the school, and I was sure we hadn't.

'What's your other name?'

'Jennifer.'

'And what's your other name besides Trays, Jennifer? You must have a *last* name. Now you tell me
what your *last* name is.'

Silence.

'Well, what's Mummy's name?'

'Mummy.'

'Mummy's got another name too. Now what do other
people call her?'

The child thought for a while, and then said, 'Angela.'

'Mummy will have another name besides Angela.

She is probably called Mrs something or other. Could you say what that other name is?'

Silence.

I asked the junior child if she knew the little one's name. She didn't. So I said to her, 'Will you please go out into the playground and ask Mrs Stubbs if she knows the name of the child she sent in.' In the meantime I carried on with my questions.

'Now Mrs Stubbs said you banged your head. Where did you bang it?'

'In the playground.'

'No, I mean where on your head. You put your finger on the bit that hurts.'

The child thought for a while, then with a tiny forefinger she touched her elbow. The junior girl came back. 'Well, does Mrs Stubbs know her name?'

'Yes.'

'What is it then?'

'Trays.'

Some twenty minutes later — having actually spoken to Mrs Stubbs and then the class teacher — I was able to write in the Bump Book, 'Thérèse Manners fell in playground and bumped head. No visible injury. Child not upset nor in any apparent pain. Mother informed by telephone.'

Sometimes a crazy and infectious sort of hooliganism seems to take over in the playground; usually on Fridays, and *always* just before holidays. My office fills with limping, bleeding, howling children. On these occasions my sympathy is limited and the first-aid perfunctory.

I once had a line-up of grazed elbows and bloody knees which were being treated on a sort of assembly-line basis. With a large swab of cotton wool and a bowl of water I was washing away blood, dirt and grit from the wounds, then clapping on a paper towel which I told the child to hold in place whilst I dried my hands and got out the sticking plaster.

144

Last in the line was Benedict who was crying noisily. Benedict *always* cried noisily. At the slightest tumble or bump Benedict always burst into tears. By the time I got through all the dirt on his knees I could find only the merest scratch, so Benedict had no sympathy from me. I slapped on all the sticking plasters then shooed the children from my office.

Benedict lingered, still crying.

'Off you go,' I said, and shoved him out through the door.

Later the teacher on playground duty came to apologise for all the injuries she had sent in.

'They're really *high* to-day,' she said. 'Oh, and were you able to do anything for Benedict?'

I was surprised at the question. 'There didn't seem to be much wrong . . . I just washed his knee, slapped on a plaster and sent him out again.'

She folded up with laughter. She laughed and laughed and laughed so much I thought I was going to have to deal with a case of hysterics.

'I sent him in,' she gasped, 'because he had something in his eye!'

When Max came to me with a nasty red weal across his neck I was about to leave the office with a pile of letters to distribute around the school. Three times I had attempted to get out of the office with those letters. The first time I had got as far as the office door when the telephone rang. The second time I had got as far as the entrance door when in came a man to read the electricity meters, and now here was Max standing in front of me, grimacing with pain.

'How did you do that?' I asked.

'Polly Hammond pulled her skipping rope across my neck.'

I wasn't surprised. Max was a playground troublemaker. He would never join in properly with any game, but wandered around the playground interfering with other children's games. He was probably deliberately grabbing at Polly's rope to stop her skipping when it happened.

The wound was quite clean so I decided to apply some Savlon antiseptic cream. I dumped my pile of letters back on the table and started scrabbling through the first-aid drawer to find the cream. It would have helped if I'd had my glasses on, but the cream didn't seem to be in its usual place. Just as the telephone started ringing I saw the blue and white tube at the back of the drawer. I squeezed out a length of cream and smeared it all over Max's weal.

'Ouch!' he yelled, 'it stings!'

'Rubbish!' I said, rubbing it in. 'It's a very mild soothing cream.'

I pushed him out of the office and answered the telephone. It must have been ten minutes later that I picked up the tube of cream which I had tossed on to the table. I was about to put it back into the drawer when the thought occurred to me that the tube looked, somehow, *different*. I put on my glasses and looked closer.

It wasn't Savlon cream. It was a blue and white tube of anti-lice hair shampoo. I read the instructions: 'Apply sparingly with liberal amounts of water. On no account use direct onto the skin.'

I dashed out of the office, across the playground and up two flights of stairs to Max's classroom.

'Just thought I would see how Max is,' I said to his teacher.

'Being a damned nuisance as usual,' she replied.

'I think I would like to have another look at that neck of his,' I said, in what I hoped was a casual, but caring sort of voice.

She was surprised – and impressed. Never before had the school secretary shown such solicitous aftercare concern.

Max, who was wandering around the classroom, seemed to be perfectly all right and he grumbled quite a bit when I insisted on taking him to the cloakroom and washing off all the cream.

'It *was* all right before you started sloshing all that soap and water over it ... and it's going down my neck too!'

Over the next few days I made occasional checks upon Max's neck. It healed up beautifully.

When it rains at playtime the children are kept in the classrooms where they are allowed to read or play quiet games. Most of them hate wet playtimes. The teachers hate them too; it means they cannot lounge for a few peaceful minutes in the staffroom. They have to collect their coffee and take it to the classroom in order to supervise the reading and the playing of quiet games.

Probably the old lady looking out from her top floor flat window hates wet playtimes. I can imagine her sitting up there waiting for the rain to stop and for the children to come out to play. But I *love* wet playtimes. I sit in the office clutching my coffee mug and looking out with happiness over the empty playground, the vacant climbing frame, and the beautiful, beautiful rain coming down in torrents.

24

Yesterday I shouted at Frederick. I am now very sorry that I shouted at Frederick because he is, really, a very nice little boy. Frederick cannot help his high-pitched screeching little voice. He probably cannot help his irritating habit of coming into the office and jumping up and down in front of me waving his arms as he screeches.

But yesterday was Monday and when Frederick came into the office just before nine o'clock I was busy receiving dinner registers, checking tins of money, giving out change to a queue of parents and answering queries about camp, music lessons and dates of the next school holidays.

Suddenly there was Frederick, leaping up and down in front of me waving his arms.

'Mrs West, Mrs West, I've forgotten my pill; I've got to have my pill at playtime and I forgot to bring it. Can I ring my Mum to ask her to bring it in? I've got to have my pill at playtime.'

I should have questioned Frederick about this pill (children are not allowed to take pills into the class-room; neither are they allowed to use the telephone except in cases of emergency). But I just wanted to get rid of Frederick. So I unburied the telephone from all the dinner registers and pushed it across the table towards him.

I was looking through the Camp Receipt book to prove to a parent that she had paid only ten pounds deposit and not twenty pounds, but there was Frederick again – now hissing at me from the other side of the table – 'Mrs West, I can't remember my telephone number.'

I don't think I sighed audibly; and I didn't say anything to him. I crossed the office (excusing my way through the thickening crowd of parents), found the card-index box, looked up Frederick's home details and called out his telephone number to him while he dialled. He must have hung on to that receiver listening to the telephone ringing out in his home for a couple of minutes. I had forgotten all about him, and was explaining to a parent how to apply for free school meals when I was aware of Frederick again; this time squeezing in behind my chair, tapping me on the arm and screeching in my ear, 'Mrs West, Mrs West, I've just remembered. My mum's gone to work today – and I've got to have my pill at playtime.'

Now, one mustn't lose one's temper with children; especially agitated children with problems. So again I got up from my desk and consulted my card-index box. I dialled the number, asked for the extension, established that I was talking to Frederick's mum — and handed the receiver to him. I presumed that he had sorted the thing out with his mother; I didn't notice him leave the office.

But ten minutes later he was back again. The office had now emptied of people, but someone had put down something sticky upon my desk (which I had just discovered with the palm of my hand) and, getting up crossly to go and wash, I had tripped over an umbrella that had been left beside my waste bin — and there was Frederick, leaping up and down and screeching, 'Mrs West, Mrs West, I've just *found* my pill . . . Can I ring my Mum again.' It was then that I shouted at Frederick.

25

Commercial Street School's official policy with regard to the taking of medicines in school is ambiguous. For many years our school booklet carried the strange instruction: 'On no account must any medicines or pills be brought into school. They must be taken to the school office.'

I have always interpreted this as meaning that we don't really approve of children being brought to school when they are in need of medicines, but that if it's terribly inconvenient for you to keep the children at home then go along and speak nicely to the school secretary and she might oblige you by administering medicines on your behalf. Consequently on my office cupboard, along with the lost property, damp swimming things, abandoned lunch boxes, footballs and odd wellington boots, you will find phials of eye drops, nose drops, boxes of tablets and sticky bottles of linctus.

Mostly the children forget to come for their medication at the appointed time (which is possibly just as well) amd those who *do* insist upon having it are usually bright enough to make sure that I am spooning the right stuff into their mouths (ears/eyes/ nose).

The LEA leaves decisions on medicines in school to the headteacher, but suggests that parents request- ing such a service be asked to sign a 'disclaimer'. (I think this is as a result of a much publicised case of a helpful but short-sighted playground lady who was carrying around a bottle of calamine lotion in one pocket and a bottle of indigestion mixture in the other. The consequences of her mistake were not disastrous to the children but were embarrassing to the LEA.)

When I was a child I suffered with the usual winter streaming colds, hacking coughs and nasty high tem- peratures when I felt absolutely horrible and didn't understand why, but I don't remember having to be at school with them. I can remember the bliss of snuggling down in bed with a hot water bottle, or sitting well wrapped up in front of the fire, with a comfortable Mum there to make me all better. But many of today's children have to be of sterner stuff. Their homes don't have comfortable mums in them. It's a case of off to school with you – and here are your nice antibiotics to make you all better.

When children are ill or injured in school most mums will come rushing along to the school when I telephone them. But some are very reluctant to do so.

'I can't take her home,' one said when I telephoned her at the school where she worked, 'there's no one there to look after her and I've got exams on. She'll just have to come back with me and sit in the staffroom until I can leave.'

Another teaching Mum was equally hard-hearted. I had telephoned her to say that her little boy seemed to have broken his arm on the football field and that Mr Masterton had taken him to hospital. She was very grateful.

'*Do* thank Mr Masterton for me – oh, and do give me a ring later on to let me know how he is.'

I said again that Mr Masterton was at that moment at the hospital and that he was expecting her to relieve him there.

'But I *can't*,' she said, 'I'm *teaching*!'

I explained that Mr Masterton had also been teaching until he interrupted his teaching to go to the football field in order to take *her* child to hospital. She finally, but with obvious surprise at my persistence, agreed to go to the hospital.

Some children, of course, are very skilled at pretending to be ill. But the teaching staff are equally skilled at spotting the pretenders and I usually assume, when a child claiming to be ill is sent to the office from the classroom, that the teacher is satisfied that the claim is truthful. If I have any doubts about the ones who look perfectly all right but claim that they 'feel sick' I make them go and sit out in the infant cloakroom in front of the sinks.

It is not a particularly pleasant place to sit, and those children who have been telling lies (and who suspect that I am *not* going to telephone their mother) soon become bored with gazing at the chipped sinks, unsavoury plugholes and grubby bits of soap. Before long they will creep back into the office saying they feel better now, and I send them back to class. The child who is genuinely unwell usually takes one look at those sinks and throws up.

Some attention-seeking children claim to 'feel sick' almost every other day. They exasperate their parents and their teachers, and I see them so many times in the office that I come to know them very well.

Alec is one of these. A bouncy little boy who lisps, he has been subjected to my 'sink treatment' on many occasions – rushing from his classroom to my office and then, after a spell at the sinks, being sent back again. But he came in recently with a note from his teacher saying, 'I think it's genuine this time.' But I doubted it – and Alec was sent out to the sinks. Within two minutes he was back.

'Mithith Wetht, I *thtill* feel thick.'

So I said that he had better go back and sit at the sinks . . . but he returned within the minute.

'Mithith Wetht, I thtill feel *ever tho* thick.'

Back I sent him again with the suggestion that he should sit there and try and *be* sick. About three minutes went by and Alec was back.

'Mithith Wetht, I *wath* thick.'

I hadn't heard a flush being pulled; I hadn't heard the tap running, and I certainly hadn't heard Alec being sick. So I looked at him sternly and asked if he was telling the truth.

He thought for a moment and then said, 'Well, it came up and it tathted like thick, but it went down again.'

So I sent him back to the sinks to have another go. Shortly after this I heard the scraping of a chair on a slate floor and a muffled banging noise coming from the direction of the infant cloakroom. I went out to investigate. With his back to me Alec was standing on his chair and looking out of the window to the playground where his classmates were filing back to their room in an orderly manner, having just finished their rounders game.

Alec, with the lavatory brush in his right hand, was banging on the window and waving his left hand energetically to his friends outside. I could hear him chuckling to himself. When I spoke to him he dropped the brush in surprise and jumped off the chair. He couldn't think of anything to say and he scuttled back to his class without argument when I dispatched him. His teacher was not pleased. Five minutes later Alec was sick in the Book Corner.

26

'Have you some string I could use for my shoes please?'

Eleven year old Sarah Percival-Flanders stood in the doorway of my office. She is a delightful girl, with a fresh clear young voice and a very direct gaze. Her manner is gentle and polite, but her voice has quite a commanding ring to it. The Percival-Flanders, who have lived for the past five hundred years in the family manor house about fifteen miles outside the city, bring their youngest daughter to school in the Range Rover. They are frequently late ('*Awfully* sorry, we've got two goats about to kid') and Mrs Percival-Flanders, who sometimes comes to the office to pay for Sarah's dinners, usually has very dirty hands ('Damned wood-burning stoves! Had to clear the whole thing out again this morning.')

The Percival-Flanders lead very interesting lives. Mrs Percival-Flanders is a professional architect. She also writes books on wholefood cookery. Mr Percival-Flanders, who is something to do with the Ordnance Survey, seems to spend a lot of the year in South America and he, too, writes an occasional book – but on travel.

The pick-up arrangements for Sarah after school are rather complicated. They involve two different sets of people and the arrangements sometimes go wrong. Mr Masterton once returned to school at 6.00 pm for a PTA meeting to find Sarah still sitting on the wall and not knowing who was supposed to have picked her up.

Although she was sitting in her usual upright and

self-contained manner, her composure was beginning to crack. The Percival-Flanders' family motto may have something about 'Endurance and Perseverance' in it, but after a wait of 2½ hours this particular Percival-Flanders had had enough. Her eyes were brimming and her commanding young voice had a waver in it.

Mr Masterton was on the telephone for twenty minutes before he was able to find out with whom Sarah should have gone home, and it took another ten minutes to arrange transport for her from one of the Percival-Flanders' many friends. (Mrs Percival-Flanders was not expected to return from a meeting in London until 8.30 pm and Mr Percival-Flanders was out of the country.)

The family's early-morning routine seems equally haphazard. As well as frequently being late, Sarah often leaves home without having had any breakfast and she comes to the office to buy biscuits before the start of school. ('Mummy forgot to get the bread out of the freezer, and we're out of cornflakes.') And now here was the child scrounging some string for her shoes.

I looked at them. She was wearing one dirty white plimsoll with a hole in the toe and one blue canvas yachting shoe which was obviously too big for her. As well as being without laces, both shoes were for left feet.

'The dog chewed up my sandals last night,' Sarah said, 'and this is all I could find to put on.'

I rummaged through the lost property and found a right foot black elastic-fronted plimsoll which was Sarah's size, and gave her a piece of string, as requested, for the plimsoll on her left foot. She went off quite happy with this solution to her difficulty.

Although the piles of lost property accumulating in my office are an untidy eyesore they frequently come in useful when I wish to provide a garment for a needy child. I have a rough and ready system for sorting it all out. Articles found lying about the school are brought into the office and put on my table. Anything unclaimed by the end of the day goes into the 'current' lost-property box.

At the end of a fortnight the contents of the current box are emptied out upon my cupboard for eventual disposal through jumble sales, Oxfam, or the school skip. It is through this pile that I rummage when the need arises. I can usually find PE shorts for any child who doesn't possess a pair and in winter time any child turning up in class wearing a thin shirt or a summer dress will be sent to me. ('Go and see if Mrs West can find you a nice warm jumper.')

One year, just before the start of the Christmas holiday, an agitated woman came into my office with two children. She started to explain to me that she had just moved to this part of the city and needed school places for her children, but then emotion overcame her and she burst into tears. She fumbled in her pocket for a handkerchief but failed to find one, so I gave her a piece of toilet paper, persuaded her to sit down and made her a cup of coffee.

The two children (a boy and a girl) stood quietly beside her with white and frightened faces. They were dressed in warm winter indoor clothes, but neither child had a coat. I knew that we didn't have room for them. Every class in the school was over-full. But I decided to let the woman tell me her story before explaining this to her.

She had left her husband the evening before. She had tolerated, she said, years of cruelty and abuse, and last night he had smashed a full bottle of milk against the wall and threatened her with the broken bottle neck. She had called the children and they had all run out of the house. She was now lodging in our local home for battered wives.

The woman talked and talked for about half-an-hour.

155

In the meantime I telephoned St Jude's, the school nearest to us, and established that they could take the children. But before they left my office I had kitted out both children with windproof jackets, woolly hats and gloves. What's more, without a twinge of conscience, I raided the current lost-property box and found a large model rocket for the little boy, and a fully dressed Victorian doll for the girl. It had occurred to me that Father Christmas might not find his way to the Home for Battered Wives.

Some of our children have become so accustomed to receiving handouts from the lost property that they come to look upon my office as a rightful source of supply. One little boy informed me recently that the swimming trunks I let him have last year are now too small, and asked if he could have another pair please. And a motherly little girl (who seems to assume all responsibility for her two younger brothers) has warned me that one of them will shortly need a larger size of wellington boots and the other could do with another pair of trousers.

Leroy, who will be leaving us this July to go on to secondary school, has been with us since the age of five. He is a tense boy who stutters and he lives with his mother in a basement flat. We never see Leroy's mother because (he explains) she has to sleep all day as she works at night. We haven't enquired what it is that his mother does at night but it doesn't seem to be very well paid because shortage of money is the reason Leroy gives for the fact that down the years his mother has never provided him with PE shorts, plimsolls, swimming trunks or towels.

Fortunately the lost property box has always been able to supply these items, along with the winter jumpers and jackets which Leroy's mum has also been unable to provide. Leroy is always late for school because (as he points out) his mother doesn't wake up and as there isn't a clock in the flat he has no way of knowing what the time is.

I understand that Leroy usually breakfasts on chocolate or crisps and lemonade, but sometimes he can find nothing at all to eat in the flat, in which case he will either do without, or take some money from his mother's handbag and buy some sweets on the way to school. Hunger sometimes persuades Leroy to come to the office and explain the situation to me. I can always provide him with a bottle of milk, and Cook will find something left over from yesterday's dinners — cheese flan, sausage rolls or date flapjacks, for example.

One Christmas Leroy had a speaking part in the school play. This was unusual because Leroy's stutter had previously distressed him to such an extent that his participation in school plays had been limited to silent walk-on parts in crowd scenes. But it was discovered that Leroy could in fact manage a sentence without difficulty provided it was spoken in unison with other children.

Thus it was that on this particular Christmas he played the part of one of the Three Kings. In company with his two classmates Leroy had to walk on to the stage, turn to face the audience and say 'We are following the Star.' A magnificent costume was made for Leroy (by his teacher) and the dress rehearsal went smoothly.

On the day of the performance (which was to be given in the evening) Leroy came to the office and, stuttering excitedly, told me that his mother was coming to watch. 'She'll s-s-see me p-p-play my p-p-part!' So far Leroy had spoken his line to an empty hall with only the rest of the class and a few teachers watching. I wondered, a little fearfully, whether he would manage it so well in a hall packed with parents — including his mother.

In the event, the Christmas play was a total success. Leroy, resplendent in bejewelled crown and flowing purple robe, strode confidently on to the stage with his equally magnificent fellow-Kings. They turned to face the audience. 'We are following the Star,' they shouted . . . with Leroy's voice ringing out loud and clear. Then they stood to one side and took their places in the tableau of other performers.

Leroy looked out over the audience. He looked along all the rows, and he looked at all the people standing at the sides and the back. Then he looked at the hall entrance door, and for the rest of the performance he continued to look at the entrance door. 'My M-m-m-mum couldn't c-come,' he said to me the next day. 'Sh-sh-she had to go out,' he explained.

Leroy, who is not particularly chatty and usually speaks only when it is necessary to convey essential information, has expressed no fears of going on to secondary school at the end of the year. But I find myself wondering whether secondary school secretaries keep boxes of useful lost property, and whether secondary school cooks are kindly people who will produce something to eat at nine o'clock in the morning. I also wonder what will happen when Leroy can find no more explanations.

Part V   Sexism, racism, and other matters of concern to the PTA

27

Being neither a parent nor a teacher my interest in the Parent Teacher Association is somewhat limited. Limited, in fact, to the evening of the AGM when the officers for the succeeding year are appointed. My first question to teaching colleagues on the morning following the AGM is 'Who was elected secretary, and can she or he type?'

From the answers I receive I can judge to what extent I am going to be bothered by requests to 'do a bit of typing' in the year ahead. So limited is my interest in the PTA that I know very little about it. I sometimes wonder who first thought up the idea of such an association and I wouldn't mind betting that it was a parent and not a teacher.

I can certainly see that a responsible, caring parent who has spent all day at home or at work in an office, shop, factory or laboratory would thoroughly enjoy an evening jaunt down to the primary school, with its stimulating wall displays and smiling teachers ready to answer all those little queries about school.

But the teachers, who have spent all day at school being smiling and stimulating must surely have to make a tremendous effort to tear themselves away from the armchair and the 'telly' to return to their place of employment. The fact that the Association has gone from strength to strength seems to indicate what a dedicated and hard-working bunch most of our teachers are.

'What on earth do you talk about?' is another question I sometimes ask, following a meeting. The replies I get are usually terse and monosyllabic. However, I gather that matters of concern like the shortage of pegs in the junior cloakroom and the date of the next jumble sale are thrashed out, and I understand that at the last meeting Ms Broughall delayed the proceedings considerably by asking why the girls' names were listed separately from the boys' names in the class attendance registers. She didn't receive a satisfactory answer.

Miss Allen mumbled something about it always having been done that way; Miss Baker said she thought it was 'more convenient for the office,' and Mr Scott, who said nothing and was probably thinking of that armchair and the 'telly', simply held his head in his hands and stared at the floor. The fact that some registers listed girls before boys, and others the reverse way, didn't satisfy Ms Broughall and I've no doubt she will soon be coming to the office to question me.

I can't give her a satisfactory answer either; and I know she will be even more concerned if she discovers that the list of children who will be transferring to secondary schools at the end of the year not only have to be separated into boys and girls for the LEA – but the boys appear on blue paper and the girls on pink.

However, if we appear to be sexist in our documentation of the children, we try to make sure that the day-to-day life of the school is above reproach in this matter. No reading schemes which show Tom helping Daddy in the garage and Sally helping Mummy in the kitchen are in use here, and our little boys enjoy cookery classes alongside the girls.

But while the staff do their best to combat sexism in school, the children, I am sorry to say, just will not co-operate. In times of classroom 'general activity' the little girls all dive into the Wendy House to busy themselves with the pots, pans and dishes, while the little boys make for the tool chest and bang away with hammers and blocks of wood.

This unfortunate attitude among our children exhibits itself at a very early age. Last Christmas I watched a group of four-year-olds assembling excitedly for their class party. The little boys were stepping on each other's toes, pushing, prodding, ramming party hats down over each other's eyes and doing all sorts of other manly things, whilst the little girls – primping their hair and smoothing their dresses – jostled for a place in front of the mirror.

I understand, moreover (from a colleague at secondary school), that the problem worsens as the children get older. Very few girls will opt for engineering (which they consider to be nasty, dirty and noisy) and no boy has yet been known to choose needlework.

Reflecting upon these matters the other day it occurred to me that there is an incidence of blatant sexism at Commercial Street School which has so far gone overlooked – even by Ms Broughall. Out in the playground are two little functional buildings; one labelled 'boys' and the other one 'girls'. What a disgrace! The notices should be removed at once. If the buildings became unisex it might, in fact, lead to better behaviour. (Little boys, under the disapproving eyes of little girls, may be less likely to do anti-social things with toilet rolls or compete with each other for the highest splash mark on the wall.)

But on the other hand, if a little boy and a little girl decide to share a cubicle, could the possible subsequent actions – taking place in privacy – be described as 'sexist'? It's all very confusing. Perhaps I should suggest to Ms Broughall that she raises the matter at the next PTA meeting.

28

Until quite recently relatively few non-white children attended Commercial Street School. But the numbers are now growing. Until quite recently relatively few white parents removed their children from Commercial Street School at the first-year junior stage to send them to private preparatory schools. But the numbers are now growing.

The significance of this trend is not lost upon Mr Masterton but he has not, until recently, considered that it is a problem. Having a strong instinctive affection for all children he tries to ensure that every child passing through his school is educated to the best of its ability and encouraged to use its talents to the full. He treats all children the same – whatever the colour of their skin.

He said as much the other day at a local conference of headteachers and was immediately dug in the ribs by a colleague alongside him who advised him to keep such remarks to himself.

'It only reflects,' said the colleague, 'your ingrained racist attitude.'

It seems that if the Director of Education had heard such a comment he would accuse Mr Masterton of ignoring the cultural diversity and varying needs of the children at his school. Whatever Mr Masterton's reply was to this statement (and I can guess it) he would not have swept aside the accusation without some reflection.

'What you must realise,' his colleague had added, 'is that we are supposed to discriminate in favour of these people.'

Leaving aside the morality, ethics or indeed wisdom of such a course of action, Mr Masterton was left with the problem of deciding *which* people. When he came back to school he disappeared into his office with the Admissions Register for a while in order to make a note of the ethnic origins of some of our children, and he reappeared with a list.

'When next you're typing out items of information for the PTA notice board,' he said, 'will you please arrange for translation to be made into Urdu, Punjabi, Hindi, Vietnamese, Chinese, Bengali and Gujarati?'

I said that he must have turned over two pages of the Admissions Register together. There could be no other reason for his seeming racial discrimination against the Turkish, Greek, French and Welsh children we had in school. Mr Masterton threw his list into the waste-paper basket, but the point I made was brought home to him the next day when we had a request from Mrs Sankey, the mother of a half-Spanish child, (I'd quite forgotten her) regarding lessons in Spanish.

Mrs Sankey was concerned that her child was speaking only English every day.

'I want my daughter to be bi-lingual,' she had said. 'My Spanish heritage should be as important to her as her Father's English one.'

She wanted the child to be released from school for one afternoon a week in order to take private Spanish lessons. Under normal circumstances Mr Masterton would have refused such a request. While sympathising with the mother's wishes he would have suggested that such lessons should take place at evening classes or weekends and should not interrupt the child's normal education.

But with the 'racist' accusation lurking at the back of his mind his cautious reply was to the effect that he would have to see if it was permissible. An outright granting of such a request would undoubtedly have encouraged other 'minority ethnic'* parents to follow Mrs Sankey's example. A situation could arise where almost a quarter of the school was attending for only nine-tenths of the academic year.

So Mr Masterton wrote a letter to the LEA School's

---

* A recent LEA instruction on terminology decrees that as the term 'ethnic minority' groups could be shortened to 'ethnics', which is offensive, the term 'minority ethnic' groups must in future be used.

Department outlining the problem and asking for guidance. We understand that his letter was passed around this department for a while and it was then decided that this was a 'curriculum matter' and the query was passed to the local Education Advisers Department. When we last enquired we gathered that a 'policy decision' was awaited. We are still waiting.

The suggestion that discrimination should be made in favour of some children in the classroom because of the colour of their skin is not one which an honest teacher would accept happily. Giving the child extra tuition is not the problem (already most of such children will receive helpful visits from a teacher from the Multi-Cultural Centre) but the maintenance of discipline *is*.

'You're only picking on me because I'm black' is a familiar resentful cry from many a black school child who has just been reprimanded. It is a cry which many teachers fear. They will abandon a few principles to make sure that such a situation doesn't arise.

Garry is a badly behaved, noisy, disruptive little boy in Mr Scott's class. ('Lively' is the teaching fraternity's euphemism for such children.) When Mr Scott was organising his Christmas play last year he made sure that every child had some part in the performance, only being selective when it came to choosing the best readers and the clearest speakers for the major parts of Mary and Joseph. Garry, along with eleven other children, had been cast as a shepherd.

But Garry objected. He wasn't going to be a snotty old shepherd; shepherds were wimps and creeps. He was going to be a king or nothing. Now if Garry had been a white boy he would have been put outside the door with his Nuffield Maths books and told to get on with that while the rest of the class enjoyed themselves with the play. But Garry is black; and Mr Scott is an ambitious young teacher. He felt that he could not risk a 'racist' smear at this stage in his career, so Garry was allowed to be a king. (The first time, so far as I know, that *four* kings turned up at Bethlehem — Mr Scott wasn't going to invoke further tears and temper in his class by shifting another child.)

Infant black children do not seem to be unreasonably resentful when corrected. I have noticed that it is only as the child progresses through the junior classes that an aggrieved attitude sometimes develops. I cannot think that the school is responsible for this change, and I wonder if the blame lies at home.

I was once showing a black lady around the school; she was thinking of placing her children with us. In one of the classrooms we entered there was a black child on its knees wiping up some spilled paint with a cloth. The lady shot out an accusing finger.

'Why is that child cleaning the floor?'

I said that I thought it was probably because the child had spilt some paint.

'Don't you keep cleaners in this place?' she snapped, 'and would you have made a *white* child do that?'

It was quite obvious that she believed we would not have. (She didn't send her children to us.)

For the time being, Commercial Street remains a predominantly 'white' school, but I think all the parents would be astonished, horrified — and even outraged — if they thought the Headteacher was in danger of being accused of having 'racist' attitudes. Mrs Slocombe, our PTA secretary, could perhaps sum up the feelings that most parents have for Mr Masterton and his school.

Mrs Slocombe has a seven-year-old girl in Miss Krantz's class and another little one due to start with us next September. The Slocombes own a large

Victorian house the other side of the river and quite some distance away from Commercial Street School. The family are not poor (Mr Slocombe is a British Telecom engineer) but they can afford only one car – which Mr Slocombe uses – and as there is no direct 'bus route between their home and Commercial Street, Mrs Slocombe hires a taxi to take her little girl to and from school.

Mr and Mrs Slocombe consider this extra expense worthwhile because they do not like their local school and are determined that their children will not attend it. The Slocombes bought their house ten years ago and have spent a lot of money on it. They live in an area of similar houses – some of which have been well maintained and some of which have not. When they first moved in, there were only a few non-white people living locally but over the years they have seen white people moving out and black people moving in.

This did not concern Mr and Mrs Slocombe until their first child was four years old and they visited their local school with the intention of registering their daughter for admission. They discovered that almost 80 per cent of the children attending the school were black, but they insist that this is not the reason for their dislike of the place. The school is new, 'purpose-built' and has first-class sports facilities, but the Slocombes found the atmosphere to be cold, tense, and somehow purposeless.

'There was no feeling of community or togetherness there,' was how Mrs Slocombe described it. The staff/pupil ratio was excellent (a limit of twenty children in each class) but the staff turnover appeared to be high. (No teacher had been at the school for more than 2½ years.) Mr Slocombe felt that the staff of the school were chosen 'politically' to ensure that there was a diversity of ethnic origins amongst the staff as well as the pupils, and that this probably accounted for the seeming lack of 'team-spirit' amongst the staff. The school – which appears to be trying to cater for a variety of cultures – was a place with no identity of its own.

This is why Mrs Slocombe takes taxi rides across the city to bring her children to Commercial Street School. The buildings may be in an appalling state of disrepair and the overcrowded classrooms may be scruffy and draughty, but Mr and Mrs Slocombe, on their first visit, immediately sensed a happy atmosphere. A shout of laughter was coming from one classroom and a purposeful buzz from another; an exciting, but disciplined game of rounders was going on in the playground – and one teacher, stapling paintings on to corridor walls, was singing to herself. This, the Slocombes decided, was the school for their children.

'I want my children to know where they *belong*,' Mrs Slocombe said. 'They are *British*! I want them to know that they have a Royal Family, a tradition of fair play – and the Church of England. Of *course* I want them to know about all these other cultures as well, but the emphasis should surely be on their *own* culture . . . the culture of *this* country. I want them to look forward to Christmas and Easter – and know what these festivals are all about. I don't want them to be schooled in an atmosphere of political tension. I want them to have a normal, traditional schooling where they respect and are fond of their teachers, and where they will accept that if they misbehave and break the rules they will be punished.'

These views must surely be held by many parents – especially those whose children are at schools where they flounder in a confusion of multiple cultures. Mums and dads up and down the British Isles will echo those words of Mrs Slocombe. But I am glad that it was Mrs Slocombe who said them, because Mrs Slocombe, her hard-working husband and delightful children are black.

29

Feckless parents, thoughtless parents, scatty-forgetful parents, and parents with peculiar lifestyles create a lot of extra work for a school secretary. A school secretary is a captive slave to do all those little things that mother forgot. She is there, at the end of the telephone, to run messages ('Please remind Hannah to go to the dentist/collect her sister from the Nursery/meet her father at Granny's') or to give again all that information she has already supplied in the form of a letter but which is now forgotten or lost ('When is the last day of term/the Easter Concert/the PTA meeting?')

A mother once telephoned me at 12.00 noon on a Friday, when I had just balanced the term's dinner account, to tell me that she was supposed to be picking up her child for lunch, but it was no longer convenient.

'I would like him to stay to school dinner,' she said. I opened my mouth to protest, but the flow of instructions had not ceased. 'Would you also tell him that Norrie is picking him up from school this afternoon, *not* Janet, and remind him to bring his jacket that he left at Norries last time.'

'Is there anything else?' I asked, sarcastically.

'Yes. He's wearing his brace; so please make sure he cleans his teeth after lunch.'

It is not only by telephone that parents command my attention. Some of them visit me. They come to the office to tell me all about it if their marriages have broken up, if they have taken to drugs, or if their children have headlice. They write to me asking about free school meals, the treatment for impetigo, or to complain about bullying in the playground.

A parent once stopped me as I was leaving school to complain about an overhanging hedge (three streets away) which was blocking the footpath and making it necessary for parents and children to walk in the road, and another parent once tapped me on the shoulder in Sainsbury's to ask what time recorder practice finished that evening and had a red bobble hat been handed in to the Lost Property box?

There are two sorts of parents. Those who go out to work, and those who don't. Each presents me with different sorts of problems. Those who don't go out to work are often active supporters of all school functions and many seem to have nothing better to do than sit at home and think of little jobs for me. They ask me to send out letters to all other parents about forthcoming bazaars or jumble sales and they ask me to be the collection point for old toys, jamjars, blankets or milk tops – depending upon which good cause they are currently supporting.

They also hold frequent children's parties, inviting lots of little ones from various classes in the school whose surnames they don't know, but whose telephone numbers they want me to supply – 'There's a little girl called Janie, and there's Marcus, Thomas and Rebecca, oh, and we must have that nice little thing with a pony tail – is it Samantha, or Jessica, or something like that? *Do* be a dear and tell me how I can contact their Mummies!'

I don't see much of the parents who go out to work. Many of them don't wish to be seen, and a few of them have children who are never allowed to be ill. A familiar sight in all primary schools is the bright and cheerful mum pushing forlorn wheezing little child through the door and saying something like 'Lydia's a little off colour today, but she loves school so much she absolutely *insisted* on coming – didn't you dear?'

And dear Lydia is given a peck on the forehead, an encouraging shove forward, and then mum makes a quick getaway. By the end of Assembly Lydia is probably running a temperature. Weeping miserably she is brought to the office, and I spend the next hour trying to trace mum who is probably tied up at a meeting, or has gone to London for the day.

Separated parents double my work. If Amy normally lives with Mum but spends the weekend with Dad (who brings her to school on the Monday) then the child will arrive without any dinner money. (I have had to wait three weeks while separated parents argue about whose turn it is to pay.) And if Amy is ill over the weekend and doesn't come to school on the Monday I must remember to tell not only the teacher but also Mum who will be furious if she turns up on Monday afternoon to collect a child who isn't there. As Mum and Dad are not on speaking terms, Dad (who doesn't like to be kept in the dark about school events) will ask me to post him a copy of every note that is sent home.

Some of our parents are not honest (during the last Open Evening we lost four staple guns and a pair of dressmaking scissors from classrooms, a radio cassette recorder/player from the hall, and a six pound joint of ham from the school kitchen 'fridge) and many of those who run into debt over dinner money are the ones with the highest incomes.

When five-year-old Dominic Hambleford was asked for his dinner money last Monday he handed over a 25 peseta piece, an American cent and 22½ pence. This, he explained, was the contents of his money box.

'Mummy and Daddy were flapping around this morning and I knew it was no good asking either of *them* for money.'

Now I know that Mummy is a GP practising at the local health centre and that Daddy is something learned at the university and he occasionally broadcasts on Radio Three. Neither parent is ever available at home so I telephoned Professor Hambleford's office at the university and left a message with his

172

secretary. I said how much I had enjoyed Professor Hambleford's recent assessment of the modern Spanish novel, with particular reference to the later works of Manuel Vázquez Montalbán, but could we have some dinner money please. I also left a message about dinner money with the telephonist at the Health Centre.

I find that this course of action is the most effective way of ensuring that my accounts balance at the end of the week. A little note of reminder sent home with the child may get lost on the way, or be forgotten about. But a message left with a subordinate at work will ensure that the correct money arrives the following day, usually with an angry letter. I don't in the least mind receiving angry letters, but I *do* mind having to carry forward arrears.

Around fifty children at Commercial Street School eat free school dinners. I suspect that at least a quarter of this number have parents who are making money 'on the side'. Mr and Mrs Flannagan are a very musical, but unemployed, young couple who are living on social security. The Flannagans have twins in Miss Baker's class and the children are brought to school on the back of Mrs Flannagan's tricycle.

Mrs Flannagan, who has long flowing black hair, cycles in bare feet and the twins are accommodated in two plastic buckets fixed either side of her rear pannier carrier. The whole ensemble looks charming, if precarious. She once came to the office wearing a full, very patched, calf-length skirt topped by a garment the like of which I hadn't seen since about 1939 – when I had been obliged to wear one. Sleeveless, collarless, strengthened with calico tape and fastened down the front with rubber buttons it was, as I remember, called a 'liberty bodice'. I said as much to Mrs Flannagan.

'Yes,' she said proudly, 'and it's an *original* one.'

I could quite believe it. Stained yellow under the arms and fraying at the bottom – it could have been the one I was last wearing in 1939. The Flannagans appear to be poor – but they are not quite so poor as the Educational Welfare Officer thinks. Every Saturday morning Mrs Flannagan (with her violin), Mr Flannagan (with his flute) and the twins (one with triangle, the other with drum) can be seen and heard at the city shopping centre.

Their music is the sort of jolly foot-tapping stuff which most people seem to enjoy. They usually have a little crowd watching them, and the last time I saw them performing I noticed that many passers-by were tossing coins into the violin case which had been left open on the ground. Mrs Flannagan saw me looking. She gave me a broad grin and a cheerful wink.

Now Mrs Creasey is not the winking type. When she needs to see me she sidles into the office with her head held to one side and an oily simpering expression on her face. Mrs Creasey has managed to convince the LEA that her little girl is entitled to free school meals but this doesn't stop the family taking an annual 6–8 week trip (usually overlapping into term-time) across Europe with their caravan.

'It's an *educational* trip,' Mrs Creasey always explains, 'Emily learns a *lot*.'

She certainly does – but Mrs Creasey would be alarmed if she knew which bits of her educational tour it was that Emily chose to talk about at school.

'Every time we go through customs I have to lie on my bunk and pretend to be asleep because all the *things* are packed underneath me.'

What things?

Emily is vague. 'Oh, just things that Daddy wants to sell in England.'

30

Who let Ms Broughall into the library? I know it is essential to have parents helping out in the library, otherwise the system would break down, but we expect all staff to exercise a bit of common sense when deciding *which* parents to ask! Look at the fuss Ms Broughall made when she discovered that the school was still using the 1611 translation of the Bible and *Hymns Ancient and Modern (Revised).* She apparently went to the PTA meeting waving both books in the air – claiming that they were racist, sexist, classist and imperialist. To let this woman loose in our library was just asking for trouble!

We are very proud of our library. True, it has been built up in a rather piecemeal fashion over the years (we rely a lot upon donations from well-wishers and an annual hand-out from the PTA) but it is a cosy place, carpeted and cushioned, where the children can browse and select books as they wish. Some of the books are not of our choice but are publications (sometimes very expensive ones) that well-meaning people have presented to us.

Sometimes these books are excellent (we now have a complete set of Collins' bird/wild animal/insect identification books); sometimes they are unfortunate (we now have four copies of the Rev. W. Keble Martin's *The Concise British Flora in Colour*) and sometimes they are highly unsuitable. (It was considered necessary to conceal in the staffroom some very 'adult' literature on male homosexuality. We daren't dispose of it yet because the child of the parent who presented it is still at school. But next year we're hoping to find a place for it on our Summer Fair bookstall.)

We prefer, of course, that donations be made in the form of cash. Then the publishers' catalogues are studied and suitable new publications are selected. We usually choose the sort of book of which not even Ms Broughall could disapprove. But we also have in our library a lot of the old favourites – and these are the ones that Ms Broughall discovered. She had no right to go prowling around the shelves. She should have been sitting at the desk and checking out the books which the children wanted to take from the library. But prowl she did; and she didn't like what she found.

Perhaps Ms Broughall is a little sensitive about the world of books (I understand that she has written 85,000 words on The Single Parent in Our Society that no one has yet published and this might explain her over-reaction). But she strode into my office, following her first day's spell of library duty, with a pile of books in her arms and the usual angry expression on her face.

Ms Broughall has a very bony face, with prominent cheekbones and a large nose. She has a mass of thinning frizzy hair and her eyes and mouth are three angry slits. When I see this face appearing around the edge of the office door my heart sinks. She always takes me by surprise. She speaks rapidly (that slit of a mouth barely moving) and the words rattle out like bullets. I can never think quickly enough to find flaws in her arguments and when she dumped those first three books upon my desk I just mumbled that I was sure Mr Masterton would consider her complaints.

After she had gone I could think of several good reasons for keeping copies of *Uncle Tom's Cabin*, *Tom Sawyer* and *Robinson Crusoe* upon our shelves, but I considered that inaction was the best way of dealing with Ms Broughall. I shoved the books onto the top shelf of my office dresser, and forgot all about them.

But the following week Ms Broughall was back again – this time with our beautifully illustrated, recently published, edition of A. A. Milne's *The World of Pooh*, together with his book of poems, *Now We Are Six*.

The books were 'classist' Ms Broughall claimed (she assured me that working class children feel 'threatened and diminished' because they don't have

176

nurseries and nannies), and *The World of Pooh* was also sexist – the only female characters being Kanga and Alexander Beetle's Aunt both of whom have minor subservient roles.

After Ms Broughall had left the office I sat reading for a while (remember that delightful chapter on the Expotition to the North Pole?), then I put *The World of Pooh* and *Now We Are Six* on the top shelf of the dresser along with the other books.

The latest book to join the pile up there is the *Collected Poems* of John Betjeman. Someone must have given us this copy and I am told that Ms Broughall had a sort of snarling seizure when she found it. She considered it to be entirely classist, partially sexist and occasionally racist. (I understand that Ms Broughall was particularly upset by verse 3 of that deliciously wickedly funny poem 'In Westminster Abbey'. If you are curious, then go and look it up for yourself. I am not prepared to risk being called a 'racist' by reprinting it here.)

Following Ms Broughall's outburst at the PTA meeting the offending copies of *Hymns Ancient and Modern (Revised)* and the Bible have been left in my office while Mr Masterton considers the matter. He discounts Ms Broughall's 'militaristic and imperialistic' criticism of the hymn book ('Onward Christian Soldiers' was one example she quoted – but the woman obviously hasn't *read* the hymn; it is all totally harmless symbolic stuff – the only enemy to be conquered being Satan) but for some time now he has been questioning the value of some of the hymns.

What, for example, does a child make of this:

Firmly I believe and Truly, God is Three and God is One, And I next acknowledge duly, Manhood taken by the Son.

Or this?

Thou spread'st a table in my sight, Thy unction grace bestoweth, And O what transport of delight, from Thy pure chalice floweth!

Mr Masterton would like to keep the good old tunes, but would like some of the words changed. He has also been considering replacing the 1611 Bible with the modern Good News Bible but in fact he has never got around to doing anything about hymn book or bible and he certainly isn't going to take any decisive action *now*. He doesn't want to give Ms Broughall the satisfaction of thinking that she had any influence upon his decision. So, for the time being the two old books stay in the office.

I was browsing through the Bible the other day when Mr Masterton came into the office and I asked him if he could remember which bits had particularly upset Ms Broughall. The sight of me sitting there so engrossed had, apparently, given him a slight shock (I suppose *any* man would feel uneasy at discovering his secretary reading the Bible in the office) and the only part he could recall from the PTA meeting was Chapter 1, Verse 5 of the Song of Solomon.

We looked it up together – 'I am black but comely O ye daughters of Jerusalem' – but we couldn't decide whether Ms Broughall wanted 'black' changed to 'white', or was it that the 'but' should be changed to 'and' or was the whole concept 'threatening and diminishing' to those of us (black and white) who were not comely?

I know that one day Mr Masterton will decide to replace both Bible and hymn book and this will mean that twenty copies of the 1611 Bible and about three hundred copies of *Hymns Ancient and Modern (Revised)* will go into the school skip, so I think I will add these two copies to the pile of saved books on the top shelf of my dresser.

Then one day, before I retire, I shall sneakily put them all back onto the school library shelves. Certainly there may be little in the Bible and hymn book which will mean much to any future browsing child (I just feel that a copy of each book should be preserved), but I am hoping that less bigoted times lie ahead of us and that another generation of Commercial Street School children will be able to follow the adventures of *Tom Sawyer*, *Robinson Crusoe* and *Uncle Tom's Cabin* and chuckle at the exploits of Piglet, Wol, Eeyore and Christopher Robin.

31

Twice a week a teacher from the Multi-Cultural Centre visits the school. The purpose of these visits (I think) is to give help to children of 'minority ethnic' origins who may have difficulty in learning because English is not their first language; also to encourage the English children to take an interest in the traditions, customs and religious beliefs of other countries. If a headteacher admits to his school a child who has no knowledge of the English language, the head is invited to seek help from the Multi-Cultural Centre – either by telephoning direct, or through the Multi-Cultural teacher allocated to his school. We understand that it is theoretically possible for a specialist in any language to come to the school to help a child, although the plethora of information which comes from the LEA about the Multi-Cultural Centre refers almost exclusively to children of 'Asian or Afro-Caribbean' origins.

However, the routine visits of the Multi-Cultural teacher to Commercial Street School seem to be based on different terms of reference. For example, we have three Asian children – Reza, Lyubov and Bijan – who never see the Multi-Cultural teacher.

They have grasped enough English to be able to 'get by' in their lessons but all three children are well below the average standard for the class. They do not see the Multi-Cultural teacher because she is with us for only two half-days a week and it is considered that other children need her time more urgently.

Reza, Lyubov and Bijan are white. However, Louis and Paulette, who are English (and were born in this city) see the Multi-Cultural teacher every week. Although they know no language *other* than English they are extremely backward and, like Reza, Lyubov and Bijan, are well below the average standard for the class. But Louis and Paulette are black. (I notice that there is another kind of one-sided benevolence operating at evening classes in this area. According to the LEA's brochure, classes in Punjabi, Sylhetti/Bengali and Urdu are free, but if one wishes to learn French, Spanish, German or Welsh one has to pay the course fee.) Nevertheless, at Commercial Street School *any* additional help is always welcome and Mr Masterton believes in using any extra pair of hands to the full.

The Multi-Cultural teacher's normal way of working with the children who need help is to withdraw a few of them from various classes and to disappear to a quiet corner (usually the staffroom) for a lesson in reading, writing and understanding English. But if Mr Masterton finds himself with an emergency on his hands (a teacher suddenly taken ill or a supply teacher late in arriving or a mess-up in the timetable which results in one teacher being responsible for two coachloads of swimmers) then, putting on his most charming smile, he will ask the Multi-Cultural teacher to dispatch her handful of charges back to their classrooms and to step into the breach.

There are sometimes a few grumbles about it being 'not my job' but so far as Mr Masterton is concerned any teacher in his school must be prepared to cope with a sudden change in role. (He would ask for their assistance only if no other way out of the difficulty could be found. Multi-cultural teachers – accustomed to dealing with only three or four children at a time, or talking to a room full of children only when the class teacher is present – sometimes go to pieces when landed with sole responsibility for a class.)

When not having to deal with demanding head-teachers like Mr Masterton, the peripatetic teacher from the Multi-Cultural Centre would appear to have a pleasant, stress-free life with few on-going responsibilities, and there is never any shortage of applicants for such posts when they are advertised in the LEA's weekly vacancy list.

On pleasant days in summer the Multi-Cultural teacher may decide to abandon the staffroom for a session outside in the sunshine. A visit to the park would be nice, so taking orange juice, plastic cups and a clutch of children she will stroll through the school gates and make for a grassy slope in the sun. Her departure may be witnessed by seven or eight teachers, some of whom will be coping with thirty or more noisy children in the stifling atmosphere of the temporary huts.

But when I once suggested to our Multi-Cultural teacher (as I handed over the orange juice and cups) that hers was an idyllic form of teaching she rolled her eyes heavenwards and said that no one understood and that she was so fed up with the damn job she was thinking of going back to nursing.

Not only did she have to put up with the irritations which beset all peripatetic teachers (no definite place in the school she could claim as her 'corner'; no one telling her in advance when the children she should be visiting had gone off to camp or on a day trip) but she also had to cope with the furious rows, constantly changing policy, disorganised and frequently dis-

181

rupted committee meetings and generally all-round unpleasant atmosphere which seemed to pervade the Multi-Cultural Centre itself.

Certainly the staff keep changing. I have lost count of the number of Multi-Cultural teachers we have been allocated over the years. With one exception they have all been white, and all but one have been female.

Mrs Hendelson was the first to come. This was in the early days of the Multi-Cultural Centre and Mrs Hendelson – a very pleasant middle-aged lady married to a clergyman – didn't seem to know what was expected of her.

'I see my role as being *nice* to these poor unfortunate children,' she once said to me, 'and I make sure they feel welcome here.'

Mrs Hendelson didn't last long.

Over the following years we had a succession of Multi-Cultural teachers none of whom I can now remember, with the exception of Miss Shepstone – and we *all* remember Miss Shepstone. Hungarian by birth she believed that children could learn only in an atmosphere of 'free expression' in music and art. This meant that every Thursday afternoon half a dozen children created an almighty din in the hall with all the school musical instruments. (The piano was broken four times during her era, and the bongo drums were smashed to pieces.)

On Thursday afternoons the staffroom became unusable because of the paint and clay which she encouraged the children to throw (inaccurately) at large pieces of card she had Sellotaped to the wall.

Mr Masterton eventually felt obliged to ask the Multi-Cultural Centre to take Miss Shepstone away. He said the school couldn't afford her. She was replaced by a black lady who was rather unfriendly and refused to join us for coffee in the staffroom. She was unreliable – rarely turning up on time and sometimes missing out odd days without explanation. She didn't return after one half-term holiday and we understand that she had complained to her superiors that she couldn't work in such a 'racist' school. This was the first indication we had that aggressive noises were coming from the Multi-Cultural Centre.

It was Mr Barker who spoke most readily about the Centre at which he was based. Mr Barker was with us for two years and he gave us a weekly blow-by-blow account of the quarrels there. He told us of committee meetings where documents were torn in two and flung across the table and where no progress could be made because of a demonstrative exodus of two thirds of the members.

'They're not interested in multi-culture,' he once said bitterly,'it's black power they want.'

Mr Barker left the teaching profession shortly after this and we heard that he now owns a very successful sports equipment shop in Colwyn Bay.

Our present Mulit-Cultural teacher is Mrs Lupin – a very enthusiastic and determined lady who knows exactly what she is doing and is perfectly capable of dealing with any black or white extremists at the Centre. She is very hard-working and cheerfully takes on all the extra tasks which Mr Masterton passes her way. It is perhaps this single-minded absorption with her work which causes Mrs Lupin to be somewhat uncaring in her appearance.

She frequently wears men's shoes – rather large and muddy ones (I get the impression that Mrs Lupin pushes her feet into the most readily available pair of shoes in the morning and sometimes it will be Mr Lupin's shoes that come to work with her) and she doesn't seem to have renewed her wardrobe since 1960 when she was probably at college. Mrs Lupin, now in her forties, is quite big in a gaunt sort of way.

During hot summer weather she will abandon her

tights and the sight of those large flat feet at the end of a pair of white, bony and somewhat battered looking legs striding out from beneath a mini-skirt causes quite a few heads to turn in astonishment and disbelief. But her broad grin and hearty laugh are always welcome in our staffroom and Mr Masterton is pleased to have her around the place.

Take last Tuesday, for example. Mr Masterton had a morning visit from a very angry mum, Mrs Hardwick, who complained to him that her child was playing exclusively with black children in the playground. She did not want her child to associate with any black children and she wished Mr Masterton to ensure that at playtimes her child was kept apart from them. A straightforward case of racism! Who better to deal with it than Mrs Lupin?

Mr Masterton left Mrs Hardwick sitting outside his office and went to the staffroom where he knew that Mrs Lupin would be. The playtime bell had just gone, and Mrs Lupin was about to have her coffee, but she plonked her mug upon the table and clumped off down the corridor without hesitation. What he didn't explain to her was that Mrs Hardwick was not only angry and determined – she was black.

'I don wan my chile to play wid dem black girls,' she had said. 'What for she tink I send her to dis school! Der's plenty of nice white girls she could play wid.'

Although most of our Multi-Cultural teachers have been very pleasant and helpful people, many of the staff question the usefulness of their visits. Children who are bright forge ahead quickly and would probably have done so without any extra help. The ones who are backward to start with often remain so throughout their educational life.

Ranjit is, perhaps, an exception. When Ranjit started with us three years ago he could speak no English whatsoever and although he has not seemed to be particularly quick in other subjects he has made startlingly good progress in reading and writing. Now a third-year infant, he can read English more fluently than any other child (black or white) in the class.

But I don't think that Mrs Lupin can claim that Ranjit's progress is entirely due to her efforts on his behalf. Ranjit has the benefit of parents who do not rely exclusively upon the State system for the education of their only son, and he gets plenty of encouragement from home.

Or, as Ranjit puts it, 'My Father; if I don't learn my words – he beat me with a stick.'

32

As the end of the summer term approaches there will be an increase in the number of parents found hovering in the corridor outside Mr Masterton's office. They are all hoping to catch him for a 'quick word'. Mr Masterton, who knows what this 'quick word' is all about, will try to avoid them. There will also be an increase in the number of teachers calling into the office. They are all hoping to have a quick look at what I have in my typewriter or on the desk.

I know what it is they are looking for and I always hide it before I leave the office. For the end of the summer term is also the end of the academic year and next September the children will all move up into different classes.

'Which class is my child going into?' is the preoccupation of the parent. 'Which children am I getting next year?' is what the teacher wants to know.

This problem would not arise at a small school where there was just one class for each age-group throughout the school. The children would progress naturally from Miss A to Mr B and so on up through the school. But at Commercial Street School we have two classes for every age group and it is Mr Masterton who decides which child goes into whose class — which is why he is pursued by questioning parents at the end of the summer term.

The determined ones will write letters. There are so many of these that I will make a file of them for Mr Masterton to study when he settles down to the job of preparing the class lists. The requests fall into three categories:

1 I want my child Dora to go into Miss Y's class and not Miss Z's;
2 I want my child Dora to go with her best friend Lizzie;
3 I do *not* want my child Dora to be in the same class as that awful boy Jacob who picks his nose and plays with himself all the time.

Mr Masterton will consider all these requests, but he is also aware that:

1 Every parent knows that Miss Y is a splendid teacher whereas Miss Z is useless and he has a pile of letters all making the same request;
2 Lizzie's mother has written a letter saying she thinks that the two girls should be separated because Dora teaches Lizzie bad words;
3 *Nobody* wants their child to share a room with that awful boy Jacob.

The teaching staff will also make suggestions: 'I think that Rupert and Horace should be split up next year; Rupert is a very bad influence on Horace, who would be quite well behaved, I think, if he was not egged on by Rupert'; or 'Alice is an extremely sensitive child. She needs a lot of reassurance. I really think she would perform much better in Miss Y's class. I don't

186

think she could cope with the rather *lively* atmosphere in Miss Z's class.'

With his file of parents' letters, a pad-full of telephone requests and a scattering of notes from teachers, Mr Masterton will start the job some time during the first fortnight in July. If he accommodated *all* the requests he would find that some teachers had all the nice, quiet, sensitive children while others had the nasty nosepickers and potential thugs; Miss Y would have 45 children in her class against the 15 in Miss Z's and about 25 children wouldn't be placed anywhere because contrary requests came from different sets of parents.

Not surprisingly, Mr Masterton sometimes gets to the stage where he sweeps aside all the bits of paper and starts from scratch to produce a set of lists that gives every teacher a fair selection of bright children and dim ones, noisy ones and quiet ones. But he knows that only a few parents will be satisfied. When the class lists have been typed and everyone has seen them there will be tears from children and sighs and raised eyebrows from teachers.

This is why I am instructed to keep the lists hidden until the last day of term. On the last afternoon the children will be told whose class they will be in next year and who will be in that class with them. And after school Mr Masterton will have to face up to a knot of very angry parents who will have assembled in the corridor outside his office door.

The end of any school term is a stressful and sometimes emotional time for all school staff and children, but until recently it was only the end of the summer term which found the *parents* getting into a state of agitation. But times are changing. The Autumn term, which traditionally ends with the celebration of Christmas, is now being complicated by parents who have something urgent they wish to communicate to Mr Masterton. In the first week of

187

October last year Mr Masterton received letters from three parents. I reproduce them in full here:

The first letter (on university-headed notepaper) came from Dr Rachel Phillpots – a rather formidable lady who is currently the Chairperson of our PTA.

To: Henry Masterton, Head of Commercial Street School.

Dear Mr Masterton,

With the term ending in almost seven weeks time you are no doubt presently deciding upon the form your Christmas entertainment will be taking this year. It is in this context I am writing to you and – having spoken to other parents on this matter – I think you can take it that my comments represent the feelings of a fair majority in the school.

Last year's end-of-term entertainment, with the Christmas readings and carols was, as usual, superbly carried out. It is always a delight to see the children performing so well and everyone appreciates all the hard work that has gone on 'behind the scenes' by the staff. But I am now wondering if the time has come for a change in the emphasis of this celebration. We are, after all, now living in a multi-cultural society and much of the significance of Christmas will be entirely lost upon children whose cultural origins are so different from our own. Historically, societies have always 'adjusted' their religious beliefs to enable a community to absorb people from other backgrounds. You will know, of course, that the early Christians celebrated not Christ's birth (which is unknown) but his epiphany to the world (Jan. 6th) and that the celebration was changed to 25th December in the fourth century when it was felt that Christ's 'birth date' should be celebrated by feasting on a date not too far removed from the pagan festival at the time of the winter solstice. And as the school's celebration has, anyway, to take place no later than the second or third week of December would this not be the opportunity to bring in some traditional festivals of other religions? I am not suggesting for a minute that Christmas should be forgotten! I think the visit of Father Christmas is a delight that all the infant children enjoy, whatever their parents' religious beliefs. But, for example, could this year the Christmas bells (which the children draw so well) celebrate instead of Christmas, the Japanese festival of Omisoka (traditionally 31st December when the bells of Buddhist temples are struck to overcome the evils of the New Year) and perhaps our candles can be lit for Hanukah (this festival recalls the re-dedication of the Temple in Jerusalem in 164 BC). The Sikh children in the school attach great significance to the 27th November (the birthday of Guru Nanak, 1469) and I think the Hindu festival of Divali (which involves the lighting of lamps and the exchange of presents and cards) is one which could well be combined with Christmas.

Perhaps you could give these suggestions some thought and perhaps discuss it with the staff at your next staff meeting. I would, of course, be delighted to give any help or advice you might need.

Yours sincerely,
Rachel Phillpots, PhD, BA, Head of Department,
Comparative Religious Studies

The second letter was from our Chairman of Governors, Major Darnall (strictly speaking an *ex*-parent: his children have long-since left primary school but Major Darnall has always maintained links with the

189

school and has served on the Board of Governors for many years).

To: H. Masterton Esq, BA, Head of Commercial Street School.

Dear Henry,

Thank you for your note. Yes, of course, I shall be delighted to act as Father Christmas again this year. Just let me know the date and time and I will make a note of it in my diary. You must also let me know the date of the plays and the carol service. These are two occasions I just wouldn't miss. I think it's marvellous the way that year after year your school produces such thumping good performances which are bright and colourful and always manage to get across the true Christian message. I know very well that all you Headteachers are under great pressure from these left-wing multi-coloured people who want to water down Christmas. (Some of them would do away with it no doubt!) We are still, theoretically, a Christian country. What do these people think the 'Christ' means in Christmas? Dash it all, we bend over backwards to let the immigrants follow their own religious beliefs (which is perfectly right and proper of course) but I don't see why we have to pretend that we haven't got beliefs of our own! It's a great comfort to know that at Commercial Street School at least the old principles and standards are maintained.

> Best wishes,
> Sincerely,
> George.

P.S. One afternoon, after school (towards the end of term) Lillian and I would be very glad if Mrs

Masterton and your goodself could join us for Sherry.

The third letter came from Angus McFarrant's father. (Angus had joined the school in September, yet Mr McFarrant (MP) had already established himself as a nuisance and a possible troublemaker. At the first PTA meeting he held up proceedings for nearly an hour because he wasn't satisfied with the school's teacher/pupil ratio on coach outings, and on another occasion he demanded to inspect a teacher's Certificate of Insurance before allowing his child to be taken to the games field by car.)

To: Mr Masterton, Head.

Dear Mr Masterton,

As this is Angus's first term at Commercial Street I don't know what your usual arrangements are for Christmas but I thought I would draw your attention to a problem which concerns not only him but quite a few other children in the school. As you know, we are atheists and for this reason I have asked for Angus to be excluded from all religious assemblies in the school. I think it is unfortunate that he is obliged to sit in the office during this time (couldn't some arrangement be made for useful instruction to be given to such children during these periods? I know that Angus isn't the only child in this situation.) I also think it is a pity that by missing your religious assembly he also misses the giving out of essential information which means that sometimes he is unaware of other (non-religious) events in the school. (Again, I would have thought that some other arrangement for the dissemination of information could be organised.) However, that is not the main point of this letter. It occurs to me that if it is your intention to hold religious festivals at Christmas then Angus, together with all the other non-Christian children in the school, is going to be excluded from many activities during the latter half of this term. I would therefore request (and I don't think, under the circumstances, that this is unreasonable) that the religious side of the festival is limited to, say, one carol concert (to take place at your normal assembly time) and that the end-of-term plays are more of a pantomime/non-religious type so that *all* children in the school can enjoy taking part in the dressing-up and acting etc. I think a visit of Father Christmas would be a good idea – and maybe a conjuror and, of course, the traditional Christmas party. I feel very strongly that so many children are excluded from so much in the school because of the pursuance of religious dogma and, especially bearing in mind the great number of different religious beliefs there are now in all schools, I should have thought that it would be a good idea to have a completely non-religious Christmas so that *all* children can enjoy it. I trust you will give my suggestion serious consideration.

Yours truly,
Hamish McFarrant

P.S. I noticed last week that the welding seems to have broken away from the wall-fixing of the handrail leading to the temporary classroom in the playground. Are you completely satisfied that this handrail is safe?

I had two suggestions to make: (1) That we cancel Christmas altogether, not even letting them have the Father Christmas they had all agreed upon; or (2) send each one of them copies of the two other letters – suggesting that they all had a meeting about it.

But Mr Masterton politely acknowledged each letter – and went ahead with organising the Festival he had been planning since the summer holidays.

Part VI Telephone bills, lavatory pans, and other matters of concern to the LEA

33

Our last telephone bill was nearly £40 more than the bill of the previous quarter and the LEA didn't like it at all. They sent us a copy of the bill with the amount circled in red and with a note attached pointing out that we appeared to have made an excessive number of calls and would we please economise in future?

The note was a photocopy, so presumably we weren't the only school to receive such an admonition, but as the telephone sits upon my desk (with just one extension to the Head) I take it that the wagging finger was directed towards me.

I reflected for a while upon the impossibility of keeping tabs on the use of my telephone (how many members of staff sneak in after school or during my lunch break to make urgent calls to their building society or British Gas? what about all those visiting contractors who want to ring 'the office'?) and came to the brilliant conclusion that it would be better if the school didn't possess a telephone.

The more I thought about it, the more the idea appealed. Why do we need a telephone? The public telephone kiosk outside the school could be used in cases of emergency and all school business could be dealt with by correspondence. I don't particularly wish to speak to the LEA and if they want to contact us (to question the accuracy of our milk return, or the staff absence sheet, for example) they can do the decent thing and write to us – thus saving money, and giving me longer to think up an answer.

Needless to say nobody else took my suggestion

seriously (although Mr Masterton could see a few advantages in being unavailable by 'phone) but I know in fact that if the school were to be disconnected from the services of British Telecom the biggest howls of horror would come from parents — particularly those with complicated domestic arrangements.

Take last Friday, for example. I was all set to make a quick getaway on the sounding of the end-of-school bell, when the telephone rang.

It was Mrs X again; and her car had broken down again.

'I'm ringing from Bath,' she wailed, 'and I can't get to school in time to pick up the children. Felicity's going to Recorders so she will be all right, and Sophia is going to Lucy's party, but Jeremy will be waiting for me and I also promised Mrs Fanshaw that I'd pick up the twins. Jeremy *could* go to Lucy's party, but I don't know what to do about the twins. Perhaps they could wait at Recorders with Felicity — but I haven't got Mrs Fanshaw's work telephone number, so would you be a dear . . .'

By the time I had sorted that lot out I knew that I had missed my bus.

I am certainly in sympathy with the LEA's desire to save money, and I don't think that my idea of telephone-less schools is any more inconvenient (for the school) than their recent idea of dispensing with the use of rooms which they describe as 'functional non-teaching space'.

It has been decided that great savings could be made if each school were to be asked to shut off one room which isn't being used for teaching purposes. The radiators are to be turned off and the cleaner forbidden to enter. Someone has apparently calculated that the savings in fuel bills alone could save the LEA several thousand pounds, but of course the real economy would be realised by each cleaner having her wages docked by X-number of pounds to compensate for the square-footage she was no longer required to clean.

For a while I was fearful of losing the use of a little room where I keep the duplicators, useful empty boxes, the school's musical instruments and unclaimed lost property, and I knew it would be useless to point out that the radiators there didn't work anyway and the cleaner never went near the place. However, the room has now been saved by the arrival of our computer which has been installed in the few square feet of space between the duplicators and the stationery cupboard.

The room now most certainly qualifies as 'functional *teaching* space'. The children have taken to the computer with knowledgeable enthusiasm and spend much of their time patiently explaining to the staff how it works. It is not the children's fault that some of the staff – particularly the older ones – are a bit slow on the uptake and have not made much use of this latest 'teaching aid'.

Younger members of staff soon discovered that the computer's ability to control children is surpassed only by that of the television set. A large colour TV set will effectively subdue and mesmerise a whole class of otherwise disruptive children. All the teacher has to do is to sit and doze at the back. A computer can exercise a similar fascination over no more than five or six children at a time, but it is not necessary for a teacher to be present.

I once went up to do some duplicating in my little room (now called the Computer Room) and found five boys seated around the computer VDU, their eyes glued to the bright images on the screen. They took it in turns to operate the keyboard; they read aloud and in unison the instructions that flashed out to them and they argued only occasionally when it was considered that the wrong button had been pushed. If those five particular boys had been left in that room without the computer I know they would have played about with the lost property, wrecked my duplicator and squirted ink all over the floor.

However, coming back to those areas of 'functional non-teaching space', I don't think the LEA realises just how useful they are to schools who have to accommodate visiting remedial teachers, psychologists, peripatetic music teachers, welfare officers and such like – all of whom require a little room to themselves.

At Commercial Street School we manage quite nicely – thanks to the good humour of all concerned. Our Medical Room also serves as a cookery classroom (and Nurse is very good about removing trays of cooling jam tarts before the medical inspection), the violin teacher uses the Reading Room (when not in use by the Remedial Teacher) and the Audiometrician will make shift with the staffroom.

But sometimes we have difficulties. Yesterday I forgot that the Education Welfare Officer had an appointment with a free-meal seeking mum and they wanted a private room for a confidential chat. I knew that classes were in session in the Computer Room and Medical Room; the violin teacher occupied the Reading Room and a helpful mum was taking a group of children for sewing in the staffroom.

The three of us wandered around the school looking for an unoccupied corner, but without success. If it hadn't been pelting with rain at the time a couple of chairs in the playground would have sufficed, but as things turned out we ended up back at the office with the two of them staring at me expectantly.

Of course they could use the office. But I knew that this mum knew that I knew that she was doing very nicely thankyou out of a boyfriend who paid for her holidays in the USA, her weekends in London and her use of a Volvo car. She certainly wouldn't want me sitting there in the office listening to her pleading poverty to the Educational Welfare Officer. So I packed up my things, switched the 'phone through to Mr Masterton and decided I would spend the last twenty minutes of the day gossiping with him.

But once again I was thwarted. There was a very tearful member of staff in his office. An intense emotional situation was obviously being investigated and my presence was not wanted. I stood in the hall for a while, watching the rain cascading in jets down the window pane from a broken guttering above, and then I did what any other sensible school secretary would have done. I went home.

I understand that during the next fifteen minutes Mr Masterton had difficulties tracing Joseph's dad to ensure that a dental appointment was kept because mum was delayed at a works committee meeting and couldn't leave, and also that Samantha's lift couldn't pick her up and could she be told to go home with Lydia, but that Lydia had already arranged to go swimming straight from school, and what with one thing and another Mr Masterton missed his appointment at the opticians and didn't get home in time to hear Evensong on Radio Three which he particularly wanted to record because an old college friend of his was playing the organ.

I may get rid of that telephone yet.

34

Near the centre of the city and occupying several acres of land are some massive grey, gaunt, concrete premises which accommodate the offices of the Local Authority. Within these premises are the people who make all the decisions about Commercial Street School. They decide how much I will be paid, how many staff Mr Masterton can engage and how many children he can admit to his school each year. They tell us how much money the caretaker is permitted to spend on cleaning materials, how many times a year we can have the grass around the school cut, and how many times a term the children can go swimming.

Most of the people who take these decisions have not set foot in a primary school since the day they left one as a child. And as most teachers, in all their working lives, have never actually *left* school it is understandable that between the administrators and the school staff there is mutual disparagement, suspicion and misunderstanding.

For example, teaching staff who occasionally visit the County Treasurer's office with a salary query come back with tales of office staff sitting around drinking tea and knitting and the entire office block glowing with warmth in winter and nicely air-conditioned in summer. At Commercial Street School we have classrooms that soar to 90°F in summer and plunge to 40°F in winter and we are all incensed by this gross unfairness.

I don't believe those stories of tea drinkers and knitters (many teachers think that no one outside their own profession actually *works*) but just in case they *are* true I hopefully comb the LEA's clerical vacancy bulletin each week to see if there is any way in which I can join them.

Between the lower orders (i.e. the clerks) of Them and Us there is less disparagement, suspicion and misunderstanding. For example, there are two very nice ladies in the 'Schools Department' (Mrs C and Mrs D) who are always pleasant, cheerful and helpful, never get in a flap and when they promise to 'ring back' they always do; then there is Mr M – a forthright, jovial-sounding man, always good for a joke; and Mrs W, who is in 'Accounts', will always patiently explain to me anything I can't understand on the Schools Capitation computer run-off.

I have never set eyes on any of these people, but over the years (through their voices on the telephone) they have become familiar friends. But these are just the few familiar voices at the offices of the LEA. Mostly the voices on the end of the telephone are unknown to me – and some of them aren't very friendly.

One of them was on at me yesterday about the weekly staff sick return. I should have posted it on Monday, but didn't get around to it. Now Monday was the day that one of the children 'accidentally' set off the fire alarm and something went wrong with the system and we couldn't turn it off – and we had all those visitors from Africa who kept asking me what was happening.

I thought of explaining this to the rather snotty female voice at the end of the telephone. I could also have told her about Henry's epileptic fit, and the twenty minutes I spent Monday lunchtime trying to get a frog out of the drain outside the kitchen – but I don't think she would have believed me.

On the other hand I do appreciate *her* problems. She is, presumably, responsible for 'processing' the staff absence forms for all the schools in the county. I can imagine her on a Tuesday morning starting to sort through the forms and finding that she can't get on with whatever it is she has to do with them because many of them are incomplete, or inaccurate, or missing. So she has to make a list of the recalcitrant schools and settle down to telephone them all before she can start work.

If the Head happens to be teaching and the secretary happens to be out of the office the telephone will be allowed to ring and ring unanswered, or the receiver will be lifted by a passing caretaker or cleaner who won't be able to help but may agree to take a message. If Commercial Street School was tenth on her list of twenty schools this week no wonder the exasperated clerk sounded a bit snotty by the time she spoke to me.

So I apologised. I could imagine her sitting there with her pile of forms. But she couldn't possibly have imagined me sitting as I was at my desk with a baby in a carry cot underneath it, a puppy tied to the table leg (both belonging to a prospective mum who was being shown around the school), a child standing beside me waiting for me to undo the valve on his trumpet and an urgent note in my hand from a teacher which read, 'Alice says she found and ate some "mushrooms" growing in the playground. Please could you go out to the playground and have a look.'

While accepting that the clerks at County Hall may be *almost* as hard-worked as I am (although certainly not so harassed), I am convinced that the officials whose duties include visiting schools work things out for themselves very nicely to ensure that their days are easy-going and stress-free.

For example, if you are the inspector responsible for investigating complaints regarding drains, central-heating boilers and internal plumbing you will arrange for yourself a programme of, say, four schools to visit in one day. First thing you will call at St Blogg's (because it is nearest to home), then on to St Cuthbert's to arrive in time for coffee (because the school secretary there is always so hospitable) and there will be just time before lunch to visit Ashmead Park.

In the afternoon you plan a longer drive out to Elmtree School, but there will be plenty of time during the day to drop in at the Comet showroom (to pick up the loudspeakers you ordered) and to look at the washing machines because it's about time the family had a new one; not forgetting to pick up the wife from the hairdressers just after 4.30 pm. A cup of tea at home, then back to the office to sign off at

5.30 pm. As the County have no intention of spending very much money on drains, boilers and internal plumbing, the reports you submit are of only slight interest to very few people.

Perhaps I am wrong. Perhaps my vision of a day in the life of a Drains, Central-heating Boiler and Internal Plumbing Inspector is totally inaccurate. But it is the only way I can account for the fact that whenever I try to contact one of them at the office I am always told that they are either 'at lunch' or 'on site' and on the occasions they drop in at Commercial Street School they are always slow-moving, convivial and relaxed – especially if it's just after two o'clock.

Officials who operate in the fringe area between the Health Service and the Education Service seem to be equally unhurried. A very nice lady comes once or twice a term to visit two children at Commercial Street School who wear hearing aids. She will report to the office at about 9.30 am and will spend a quarter of an hour bringing me up-to-date with the two case histories before going to see the class teacher of the first child.

There will be an in-depth discussion on the child's progress in class, followed by the child being taken away to a quiet corner for a long talk and a hearing test. At coffee time Mr Masterton will find himself listening to an earnest re-appraisal of the first child's progress, and the second child's teacher will be then approached and the procedure repeated.

At the end of the morning the hearing impaired children's visitor will return to the office to fix up with me the date of her next visit. The speech therapist, who comes every month, is having marriage problems. She tells me all about them each time she visits. The audiometrician is looking for a cottage in the country, and the educational psychologist (who is in the menopause) is looking forward to retirement. All these pleasant people seem to have so much *time*. They like to sit in the office and chat — and they don't seem to notice that *I* haven't time to listen.

Excluded from this bunch of visitors with undemanding jobs is the school nurse who is overworked and under constant pressure from the Area Health Authority on one side and headteachers on the other. Nurse comes twice a week to Commercial Street School and she always has a tight programme planned of the children she must weigh, measure and eye-test before the next medical inspection — with a few follow-up jobs on children with problems. She will always be met by a welcoming Mr Masterton who says how pleased he is to see her, and who then lists all the little problems he would like her to have a look at.

Last week it was Zoe's septic finger, a nasty burn mark on Jason's arm, and all the heads in Miss Baker's class because several mothers had complained that their children had head lice.

The Area Health Authority has recently told all the nurses in this area that they are not to do first aid in schools nor make routine inspections of heads — but I have never known a nurse to refuse. Our nurse co-operates patiently with all Mr Masterton's requests — and if necessary comes back to do unpaid overtime in order to complete her routine 'surveys'.

I am supposed to make a note in the School Log of the names and official positions of all the visitors to the school, but there are so many of them that I frequently forget to do so; only the most important or unusual visitors are noted. The two officials who make the most impact on schools, and whose visits are remembered with awe for many months afterwards, are the Home Office inspector and the LEA's accountant.

We once had a Home Office inspector unkind enough to telephone the school on the second day of term to give us twenty-four hours' notice of his intended visit. None of the classes had work prepared. The walls were bare and no projects had been started. I don't think that any of the teaching staff had much sleep that night. I wasn't in the least bit worried. Home Office inspectors are not interested in the school office.

However, the situation is reversed when the accountant visits because he spends all day in the office going through my books and counting the cash. The rest of the school carries on normally and they all wonder why I'm in a flap.

We once had an accountant unkind enough to visit on the last day of the Easter term. I had just two hours' notice and was at least able to make sure that the petty cash balanced and I dispatched the caretaker to the bank with all the music cheques which should have been banked the previous week. For some reason my school dinner tin contained £5.97 too much. I hastily transferred it to the Ethiopia Famine Relief tin before he arrived.

It is unusual for visitors to call on the last day of term and, fortunately, I have never known anyone from outside the school to visit on the last day of the Christmas term. We are not fit to be visited on such a day. The classrooms will be a chaotic mess of stripped paper trimmings and dismantled cribs and Christmas trees; I will be drinking the last of the staff Christmas luncheon wine as I balance my accounts; Mr Masterton will be strolling around smoking his pipe; the kitchen staff will be deciding which of them takes home what leftovers, and the caretaker (if we currently have one) will be drunk.

But the approach of Christmas will be celebrated at County Hall too. I have seen paper trimmings hanging in the windows of those gaunt concrete walls, and I can imagine the scene inside. The knitting will have been put aside; the cups will contain something stronger than tea, and even in the accountant's department there may be a funny hat or two to be seen. But I bet the Inspector of Drains, Boilers and Internal Plumbing won't be there. He will be out 'on site' – fetching the Christmas tree, ordering the turkey and (if it's after two o'clock) driving around at a very careful twenty miles per hour.

<h2 style="text-align:center">35</h2>

I am sure that so far as Elspeth was concerned the most important thing about that Friday was that she had been allowed to take her Strawberry Shortcake doll to school. She had it clutched in her hand as she filed out with the rest of the class at playtime. Elspeth's class occupies the classroom above my office and every playtime and dinnertime I hear the trundle and scuffle of thirty little pairs of feet going up and down that staircase.

It is a handsome staircase, constructed 110 years ago by one Matthew Grimshaw, an energetic Victorian builder who was responsible for the construction of most of the houses in this area. Whether Grimshaw himself constructed the staircase (or, more likely, one of the craftsmen employed by him) is not recorded, but the designs of all his staircases are somewhat similar.

A reasonably broad and substantial wooden stairway is made to look wider and even more substantial by the attachment of pieces of wooden moulding to the stair ends and tread edges. The moulding nailed on the stair ends serves not only to make the stairs look wider; each strip of moulding also supports an ornate, cast-iron baluster which is attached to the moulding by two short screws – a third screw going into an ornate piece of wood which is attached to the stair ends underneath the piece of moulding. Each piece of cast iron (weighing about 28lb) is attached to the handrail by one obliquely-angled screw.

Grimshaw no doubt considered that his staircase was sound enough and, as it has survived several generations of family use, two world wars and finally sixty years of the scuffling feet of schoolchildren, who could disagree with him? But each Grimshaw bit of moulding had now been supporting 28lb of cast iron for 110 years; the screws to the handrail and moulding were rusty and tired and crumbling. The two Grimshaw nails which held each piece of moulding against its stair end had also rusted and the moulding was gradually easing itself away.

None of us noticed any of this. I used to run up and down those stairs many times each day without looking at the balustrade. If I had given it any thought (and I didn't) I would have assumed that the weight of each piece of cast iron was in fact being taken by the whole stairway. None of us knew about those pieces of moulding that were gradually being prised, by rust, away from the staircase. Not until play time on that Friday.

Mrs Lloyd is the teacher in charge of the class above my office and every playtime she ushers the children down that staircase and out into the play-ground. The children are aged between five and six years and Mrs Lloyd does not allow them to run down the stairs. She leads them in single file from the classroom along the landing and down the stairs. She then stands at the foot of the staircase and watches the children filing down; each child walking alongside the balustrade; each child catching hold of each piece of cast iron on the way down.

If the children had noticed that some of the fancy iron bars had become wobbly, it would not have occurred to them to say so. For all they knew fancy cast-iron bars were *supposed* to wobble. One of the balusters had become particularly wobbly; it was the one up on the landing just at the head of the stair-case. Elspeth, who was near the front of the line of children, would have noticed it wobble as she touched it but she went on down the staircase and passed in front of Mrs Lloyd – the line of children doubling back in the hall to walk alongside the stairway on their way towards the original back door of the old house.

By this time the class on the ground floor was also leaving its room and the hallway became filled with jostling, chattering children, making their way out to the playground. Elspeth had just reached that spot in the hallway underneath the stair-well and imme-diately below the wobbly baluster above when the twenty-fifth child in the class touched it and the fancy cast-iron baluster, still attached to the piece of moulding, fell away.

Elspeth couldn't have known what had happened above her. She was more concerned with the fact that Adrian James, from the other class, had grabbed her Strawberry Shortcake doll from her, and in tussling with him to get it back she leaned slightly to one side.

It came down like a pile-driver. I heard the bang from my office. I had never heard a bang quite like it; it was more like an explosion. When pictures fall off walls, when cupboards are pushed over and when children fall down stairs there are always loud bangs – but *those* bangs are muffled at the edges, with rumblings and rattles and are quite often followed by a howling cry from a child. This bang was not muffled at the edges and no child cried. When I heard Mrs Lloyd shriek I knew that something dread-ful had happened.

It missed. Elspeth's fight with Adrian James took her away from the direct line of the falling cast iron. One edge of the wooden moulding caught in her pocket and ripped it from her billowing dress. The piece of cast iron hit the hall floor with such force that an ornate knob which protruded from the bottom embedded itself in the floorboards, and the baluster, with the pieces of moulding still attached, stood solid and upright in the hallway. Elspeth looked at it with surprise and then started giggling. Mrs Lloyd fainted.

The news soon became widespread that a child attending Commercial Street School had nearly been killed by a piece falling from a balustrade. The Chairman of the PTA demanded to see the County Surveyor; a special meeting of the Governors was called for; questions were asked by our local councillor at the next Schools Re-building Planning Committee and the school received many visitors from various departments of the LEA. They all came to stare with solemn faces (and blank minds?) at our Victorian staircase; some of them (presumably to demonstrate their practical knowledge and ability) occasionally poking at and shaking the remaining balusters.

Who was to blame? The Health and Safety Department were quick to refer to correspondence (of several years ago) in which the responsibility of checking up on potential hazards in the school was placed firmly upon the headteacher. The Head had been instructed to make a termly inspection of the premises with the caretaker and to report to the LEA any potential danger areas. But who would have suspected the balusters?

The questions and answers flew between the School and the Health and Safety Department. Why didn't the cleaner notice the loose balusters when she was cleaning them? Which cleaner? We were unable to keep cleaners for long and, anyway, with the cut-down of cleaning hours the cleaner barely had time to clean the classrooms and the hall without ever getting around to cleaning balusters! How many more bits of the school had to fall off (the PTA wanted to know) before the LEA carried out any maintenance? What about the crumbling stonework and loose roof slates – was the Head supposed to check up on those things with the caretaker too?

The LEA claimed that it had neither the time nor the money to conduct routine inspections and maintenance of all school properties but – presumably to make sure it could carry no blame for this particular incident – a statement was issued to three local newspapers claiming that the baluster screws had been 'tampered with'.

The children, it seemed, knew nothing about all this furore. We hope that they had forgotten all about the falling baluster by 'going home' time on that day. I don't think Elspeth mentioned it to her mother (who probably assumed that the torn pocket was the result of a playground game) and no one on the staff has mentioned it to Elspeth's mother. No doubt she heard all about the falling baluster, and must have tut-tutted along with all the other mothers. But she didn't know, and hopefully she will never know, that on that particular Friday Elspeth's little head, with its glossy chestnut hair, was within inches of being smashed to pieces by 28lb of rusty Victorian cast iron.

36

Protruding from the outside wall just underneath my office window there is a dribbling tap. I reported this dribbling tap about eighteen months ago but am now very pleased that nothing was done about it because the muddy piece of ground outside my office window contains a tangle of overgrown holly, bay and elder trees, all of which attract birds who are grateful for the large permanemt puddle created by the dribbling tap.

Moreover, the plumbing connected to the dribbling tap must travel somewhere near the school boilers because I notice that as soon as the central heating system is in operation the tap dribbles warm water. Last winter, when the outside temperature had been well below freezing non-stop for several weeks, I was delighted to see a small group of fieldfares, redwings, blackbirds, song thrushes, a robin and several species of tits, queueing up for a warm drink.

Things like dribbling taps, broken lino, faulty lavatory cisterns, loose doorknobs, broken sash cords, leaking roofs, blocked drains, broken fences and crumbling walls are reported to the Local Authority as a matter of routine and, as a matter of routine, they are usually ignored. The only way we can be sure of getting any action is by putting the report in writing and stating that the condition is highly dangerous (thereby firmly passing the buck) and threatening to close the school.

The Local Authority is extremely sensitive to matters of health and safety.We recently had all our lavatory blocks painted (we had been requesting this for about seven years) because an outbreak of dysentry at a couple of schools in this area had received a lot of publicity in the local newspapers and on local radio. There are a lot of lavatories at Commercial Street School, and the painting of them all was quite a long-drawn-out exercise.

To the children's delight two Portaloo cabins were plumbed into the playground (girls and boys spent most of their playtimes queueing up in order to use them) and the staff were invited to choose a new colour scheme for the toilets.

No one was prepared to give the invitation serious consideration and the suggestions ranged from 'sludge brown walls with black skirting boards' (mine) to 'easy wipe-over William Morris designed wallpaper' (Mrs Snow's) but in the end patriotic hilarity won the day and our lavatory blocks are now resplendent with red doors, white skirting boards, and blue walls. (How long, I wonder, before we receive a complaint from the Multi-Cultural Centre?)

Unfortunately such was the LEA's urgency for getting this job done they didn't wait to attend to some necessary roof repairs first and the pretty blue walls in two of the toilets are now stained with brown dribbles and black mould.

Shortly after this lavatory painting episode we had an unexpected visit from an inspector of the Buildings Maintenance Department who told us that there was a little bit of money left over for school redecorations and he asked if there was something else we would like done. For some strange financial reason, however, the work had to be completed before the end of the financial year even if it meant the contractor working through the Easter holidays.

Although taken by surprise Mr Masterton was able to decide instantly that his office, my office, the entrance hall and the dining hall should be the areas to receive this bonus treatment and the inspector of the Buildings Maintenance Department went away promising immediate action.

He was telling the truth! The day after his visit we had a little man on the doorstep clutching books of wallpaper samples and paint shade cards. He was a local contractor who had been asked to give the Buildings Maintenance Department a quick quote and to prepare to get started on the job immediately.

He was with us all morning. He measured the rooms, we chose our wallpaper, and I worked overtime that evening packing away loose files and bundles of paper into boxes ready to evacuate my room.

'I'd like to start work in three days' time,' the little man had said. But we never saw him again.

For the following week I worked out of my cardboard boxes, and then eventually dumped the files and loose papers back on to my cupboard and refilled the pigeon holes in my dresser.

The Easter holidays came and went. The dining hall, entrance hall and the two offices remained undecorated. Several weeks into the summer term I rang the Buildings Maintenance Department and asked about this delay. I was told that they had 'run out of money' and that the work could no longer be authorised. However, Mr Masterton, who on the strangth of having his office redecorated had persuaded the Supplies Department to allocate him a new carpet and two new fabric-covered arm chairs, complained loudly in high places and eventually achieved a redecorated office.

But not without some jiggery-pokery. The contractor who came to do the job had on his worksheet the instruction 'redecorate school kitchen'.

'It's the only way I could get the money authorised,' the man from the Buildings Maintenance Department had said with a nod and a wink. 'They never refuse money to decorate a school kitchen because of health and safety.'

Because of health and safety we receive frequent (and surprise) visits from the Fire Officer. And he's always very cross with us. He's cross because of all the spare paper, drama costumes, scenery and the useful (but very combustible) bits and pieces we store in the attics. He's cross because of the fire doors we prop open (teacher wishes to see what the children working in the corridor are up to) and he's cross because we remove all those nasty door closers.

Door closers are fine things provided you are a fit and healthy adult with a strong arm. But when you are a five-year-old child wishing to get out of the classroom to go to the toilet or back into the classroom having returned from the toilet, a door fixed with a spring closer can be an unmanageable and distressing obstacle. So we remove them. When the

215

fire officer calls we apologise guiltily and the door closers are fixed into position once more. When he's gone we remove them again.

No doubt the fire officer considers us to be irresponsible and uncaring towards matters of fire precaution but *he* overlooks the biggest fire hazard in the school – the fire alarm system. The fire alarm at Commercial Street School is an ear-splitting (and, in my opinion, brain damaging) cacophony which shrieks into action four or five times a term. So far there have been four different reasons for the operation of the fire alarm:

1   the fire practice (which takes place once a term in the week preceding the meeting of the school Governors);
2   a child breaks a 'safety' glass for a prank,
3   contractors working on some electrical fault in the school accidentally set the thing off; and
4   the termly visit of the fire-alarm servicing contractor who always says that his 'test' won't involve actually sounding the alarm, but it always does.

We are prepared well in advance for reason (1) and the children file out obediently to their allotted places in the playground. At all other times when the alarm sounds we assume that it is doing so for reasons (2), (3) or (4), and we all ignore it.

Matters of health and safety notwithstanding, it seems that all local authorities are reluctant to spend money upon the maintenance of school buildings, and those of us who have to work in them have come to accept, as normal, conditions of dirt, damp, draught and decay which would not be allowed to exist in any establishment protected by the Shops and Offices Acts.

So inured are we to our surroundings that we don't

always realise how scruffy and downtrodden the school must appear to outsiders. After all, the crumbling plasterwork is usually covered by the children's delightful paintings; 'interesting' bits of pottery are displayed in alcoves in the entrance hall, and Miss Krantz and Mrs Snow do very clever things with draped handwoven material and vases of flowers.

But an opportunity to see our school as it really is came recently when Mr Masterton was approached by a firm of aerial photographers who had been operating in our part of the city. Would we like a large print of our school as viewed from above? What a good idea! We could have a few hundred smaller copies and sell them as novelties at the next Summer Fair!

But Mr Masterton changed his mind when he saw the proof. It wasn't so much the broken slates and crumbling disused chimney pots that worried him, but all those clearly revealed squalid little corners where a succession of caretakers had dumped the broken chairs, bits of wire, battered milk crates and abandoned buckets. The skip and rubbish bin area (neatly concealed from passers-by with some lapboard fencing) was now on full view – a shabby overflowing mess towards one side of the photograph. Some large, hideous and obviously homemade 'disco' loudspeakers which some well-meaning parent had presented to the school were only half-buried in the skip and quite clearly identifiable. The proof was quickly torn up and thrown away.

But something else was revealed upon that photograph which I found encouraging. There were a lot more trees and bushes in and around the school than I had realised. This inner-city area of dereliction was filling up with foliage. And I was delighted to see that along with the half-bricks, milk bottles and footballs lodged in the roof gullies and gutterings of the school there were at least five mature buddleia bushes growing.

37

The LEA has recently changed its policy with regard to the treatment of headlice – and it's all rather worrying.

The matter is of particular concern to school secretaries because it is to the office that children are sent if they are considered to be unfit to sit in the classroom – and while (at Commercial Street School) a few heads with a sprinkling of nits can be tolerated in class for the time being, a head well stocked with crawling things (that occasionally drop out upon exercise books) will be banished forthwith.

The afflicted child is sent along for me to accommodate, along with the nose bleeders, the incessant coughers, the sore throaters and those 'not feeling very well'. Sometimes my morning sick parade is a mild affair, with just the odd child sitting whimpering in the corner waiting for Mummy to collect. Other times it is more dramatic – like last Friday, for example, when seven-year-old Rebecca came to my desk and leaning over it weakly said, 'I feel sick.' And she was.

However, mopping up all these messes in the office and keeping out of direct range of the coughers and sneezers is an everyday feature of the school secretary's life, and most of us develop a phlegmatic attitude and an immunity to infection which carries us happily through each day. But I have never heard of anyone being immune to head lice.

In her twice-weekly visit our school nurse used to include head inspection along with the eye test and weight checking. Any child found with nits was given a bottle of lice-lotion to take home, along with a letter from nurse and a printed sheet of instructions. Children with head lice walking about upon their scalps were isolated from the rest of the class. Parents were contacted by telephone (if possible) and asked to take the child away from school immediately – along with a bottle of lotion, spare supplies of which were always kept in the office. Usually the parents co-operated with this treatment, except for the occasional awkward family like the Thomas's.

Mrs Thomas, a gentle person given to meditation and vegetarianism, subscribes to a sanctity-of-all-life point of view, and when the Thomas twins were removed from class because of the exuberance of life upon their heads Mrs Thomas agreed to take them home but refused the lotion. On no account would she chemically exterminate the headlice (she explained to Nurse and me), she would remove them with kindness and persuasion. Greatly intrigued, I asked for more details and Mrs Thomas obliged.

Certain *meaningful herbs* would be gathered from the garden, she said, and placed in two plastic bags which would then be put over the children's heads and held in place by elastic bands. The children would wear these bags for several hours and then they would sit holding hands with Mother whilst she 'communed' with the headlice and explained to them that they were not wanted in the hair.

The children would then be taken to the garden where the bags would be removed and the contents – herbs with lice attached – emptied into the flower borders. Nurse, who has been with us a long time and has seen and heard everything, said she didn't mind in the least what method Mrs Thomas used to remove the lice, so long as it worked.

But on this occasion, however, there appeared to be a breakdown in communication between Mrs Thomas and the headlice who either didn't understand what was required of them, or didn't like the look of

219

the Thomas's back garden, because when the twins returned to school the following day a quick inspection in the office revealed the lice as unrepentently present as before. Mrs Thomas was again summoned and this time she admitted that sterner action was called for. The whole family would travel to Bradford to consult their Guru.

The Thomas twins were absent from school for the following three days and it was obvious upon their return that the Guru had succeeded where Mother had failed (or was the Bradford back garden a more acceptable habitat?) because the Thomas twins' hair was shining and louse-free. (But by this time, however, the rest of the class were scratching.)

Parents' attitudes to headlice upon their offspring differ tremendously. Some are lightheartedly hearty as they come to the office to collect some lotion ('Alice had headlice would you believe! Better let me have three bottles; might as well treat the whole family while we're at it!), while others wait until the office is empty of other parents before they creep in, furtive and furious ('Our Kevin's got *Things* in his hair! He must have picked them up from someone else in his class. We never had this trouble at his last school!')

But at least the problem was reasonably contained, so long as I had lotion to hand out ad lib and so long as the parents were prepared to use it. But now the LEA has changed its policy – deciding that the curtailment of this nuisance should be the parents' responsibility and not the school's.

A few weeks back we had an Operation Head Hunt in all the schools in this area, when teams of nurses and their assistants systematically inspected all the children's heads; segregated those with lice, ensured that the parents treated the children's heads, and did a follow-up inspection just to make sure.

All parents then received an illustrated and comprehensive booklet giving basic information upon ead care and the eradication of lice, and telling them that in future it was up to them. There would be no more routine inspections of heads, and no more lotion held in school. They were advised to apply for help to their nearest health centre.

That's all very well, but it's so much simpler to pop into school than to trail along to the health centre, isn't it? So some of our mums aren't bothering; and some of our children are scratching again; and all of them are being sent along to the office again, but there's not a drop of lotion here. The cupboard is bare – which is why you find me sitting here with my head in a plastic bag filled with *meaningful herbs* and secured with an elastic band.

38

Tracey Perkins and her dad stood in the office while I explained to them all about PAL. Tracey Perkins, who is eight years old, had a dirty face and a cold sore and was wearing a torn plastic mac that was several sizes too small for her. She edged across to the gas fire as I was talking and she held out her hands – very thin, purply-red hands – to the warm air.

Her Dad (who had recently come to this city from Bolton in search of work) was lodging at our local hostel for homeless families and wanted to register Tracey for school. But he couldn't, I said, because of PAL.

The Local Authority's Planned Admission Level for our school was no more than 30 children in any one year group, and as all our classes now had 32 or 33 children we were not allowed to admit any more. Mr Perkins would have to write to the Education Office, I explained, and they would put his case before the next Appeals Committee (which meets every fortnight) and they would no doubt agree that, on 'social' grounds, PAL should be waived in this instance and that Tracey should be admitted to Commercial Street School.

Mr Perkins was angry and confused. He didn't want to know anything about PAL. The job he had come for had fallen through; his wife had left him and he had been kicked out of his flat. All in all his life was in a mess and he just wanted to get Tracey into school while he sorted things out.

'It's the law innit!' he said. 'She's gotta be educated!'

I wrote down the name and address of the Director of Education for him and he went off clutching this bit of paper but muttering in disbelief.

We've had a lot of trouble with PAL all this term. Last week it was an exasperated Mrs Harrowes in my office who had brought seven-year-old Gideon to be registered. Gideon, who was dressed from curly head to wellington-booted toe in a 'fur' lined 'thermal' outfit, crawled around the office floor, pushed over the wastepaper bin, and then amused himself throwing his sheepskin mittens in a vain attempt to dislodge a left-over Christmas balloon from the top of my dresser.

'But this is ludicrous,' Mrs Harrowes protested. 'We've just bought a house within walking distance of this school . . . and anyway, I understood that all schools were in a falling-roll situation!'

I said that I didn't know about other schools but such a state of affairs did not apply to us. We were in a three-to-a-desk-and-take-it-in-turns-to-sit-in-the-corridor situation, and I suggested that she wrote to the Director of Education.

Grabbing Gideon away from my typewriter (where I later discovered his mittens, shoved into the well of the type-basket) Mrs Harrowes stormed out. But Mrs Harrowes didn't really need my advice; she knows exactly what to do. Mrs Harrowes will not only write to the Director of Education, but also to the Chairman of Governors and her local MP.

I've no doubt at all that within three or four weeks we shall be putting another desk in the corridor and making room for Gideon. What's more, we will make room for Tracey too – if ever her dad gets around to complaining officially, because the astonishing thing about PAL is that, when challenged, the LEA has *always* to withdraw its objections 'on social grounds'. Our neighbouring schools are also over-crowded but, as Tracey's Dad put it, the children have 'gotta be educated'.

But I doubt if we shall see Tracey again. I don't think her dad goes much on writing to directors of education. I've a shrewd suspicion that after kicking his heels for a week in the hostel for homeless families Mr Perkins will say sod PAL and will set off back to Bolton, dragging Tracey behind him. (But at least her hands won't be so cold on the homeward journey; I gave her Gideon's mittens.)

39

Another private school prospectus has arrived today. These prospectuses start coming immediately after Christmas – large glossy brochures containing infor-mation about fees, entrance examinations and including a sheaf of application forms to give to any interested parents of fourth-year junior children.

This latest prospectus is very impressive. The cover has a tasteful design, bearing the school crest and motto on the front and a photograph of the Head on the back. He is sitting at ease behind his desk; shapely hands resting together lightly upon his blot-ter. The correct amount of shirt cuff is showing.

A handsome man – in his early forties I would

guess – his hair waves smoothly to ear level. His smile is friendly, boyish and middle class. I have spoken to him (once) on the telephone. He has a fresh, bright, Radio Three sort of voice which matches his smile.

This brochure has many photographs inside. There is a summer scene across the school playing fields; young men dressed in creamy-white trousers and shirts are playing cricket. To one side is the pavilion; to the other side a corner of the school buildings (sixteenth-century with Victorian and later additions). There is a fringe of poplar trees at the edge of the playing fields and overhead a great summer sky of blue with billowing white cumulus. The photographer had chosen his moment well.

Other photographs show the students at work – in the library, the laboratories and in front of banks of computers. The students – all with earnest, self-assured faces, wear school uniform in the library, white coats in the laboratory and they work in short sleeves before their visual display units. There are four girls amongst them (reflecting a recent change in the school's admission policy) and one black face.

Mr Masterton, as a committed state-school comprehensive system man, flips through these brochures tut-tuttingly, then throws them into the wastepaper bin. The gesture fools no-one. By the time our children have reached the fourth year junior stage, Mr Masterton knows each one of them very well. And I know (and he knows that I know) that he has already identified these children whom he considers to be 'private sector material'.

If the parents of these children do not approach him for advice he will very cautiously suggest to them (during a private chat) that their child is worthy of admission to such and such a school and could, without doubt, pass the entrance examination. Last year 25 per cent of our fourth-year children went on to private-school education – and many of them had won scholarships. The figures for this year will reflect, I think, a similar pattern.

Mr Masterton is proud of and pleased with every child in his school who tries hard and succeeds – whether that child is very backward and just manages the basics of reading and writing by the time it leaves, or whether it is brilliant and obviously destined for a career in high places. When it leaves Commercial Street School, each child must be pointed in the right direction – and different children need different directions.

The left-wing members of our school governing body are not pleased with the yearly statistics which show an increasing number of Commercial Street fourth-year children moving to private schools. But Mr Masterton is indifferent to their displeasure. The private school headteachers send him invitations each summer to coffee mornings or sherry evenings. He politely declines them all.

Although most of the children attending Commercial Street School do so because it is their nearest school, Mr Masterton's growing reputation for producing scholarship children has meant that parents from distant parts of the city often try to register their children with us. The limitations imposed upon us by PAL theoretically protect us from being swamped by the children of ambitious parents, but in fact we find that PAL is only a slight hurdle to any determined and articulate parent who has influence in the right places.

Furthermore, having secured a place at Commercial Street School, determined and articulate parents can maintain that place even though it may occasionally suit their purpose to break a few of the attendance rules. For example, if a child is absent from school during term-time for more than a fortnight (for any reason other than illness) that child's name has to be removed from the register. That is the rule of the LEA.

At Commercial Street School, where there is always a waiting list for all vacancies, this usually means that the child loses its right to attend the school again. It is a rule which Mr Masterton frequently ignores because many of our parents are unable to take their annual holidays during the school holidays. But while he is quite happy to turn a blind eye to an absence of three weeks or even a month he felt unable to bend the rules for Mr Bonnet who wanted to remove his daughter Emma for a year.

Mr Bonnet's reasons were not frivolous. His employer wished him to transfer to Scotland for a year and was able to provide a flat for his family. As the Bonnets were currently living with Mr Bonnet's parents he felt that a year's break would be good for them all, but at the end of the year the family would be returning to live at the same address until such time as he could buy his own house. Emma Bonnet was coming up to the last year of the infants stage and Mr Bonnet would like her to rejoin the school at the first-year junior stage. Mr Masterton explained the rule to Mr Bonnet and said he would be delighted to have Emma back in a year's time – provided there was room for her.

Not long after this Mr Masterton was trying to explain the same rule to Professor Mantleson and his wife who wished to take their two children with them to Australia for a year. Professor Mantleson was taking part in an exchange visit to the Australian National University at Canberra and thought it would be a marvellous experience for his wife and two boys to come with him.

Mr Masterton agreed with him – but when he explained that the children could not be guaranteed places back at Commercial Street School on their return the professor and his wife were shocked and disbelieving. Mrs Mantleson's first reaction was to consider cancelling her trip with the boys, but then she had a better idea.

Three weeks later she came to my office triumphantly waving a letter the Mantlesons had received from the Director of Education himself. *Of course* Mrs Mantleson and the boys should accompany the professor, the Director had said, and they could certainly be assured of places for the boys at Commercial Street School on their return.

Determined and articulate parents may be well equipped to challenge the LEA's admission policies (and provided they remain vigilant throughout their child's school life they can ensure that their child receives the best education that is available within the state system) but if they have a high income *as well* then all educational problems can be neatly side-stepped. The private schools are there, with open doors, and offering excellent facilities.

Some of them now accept children at the 'rising five' stage and all of them admit children at any age thereafter. Some parents leave their children in the State system for almost all of their school life – only transferring to a private school for the last year or two if they discover that the State system doesn't offer adequate education in a particular subject at the sixth-form stage.

An American lady came to my office a few days ago. Her husband had come to Britain to work; they had just moved into our area and she wished to register her six-year-old boy for admission to Commercial Street School. We do not have room for another six-year-old child and once again I found myself explaining the overcrowded state of the school, the LEA's policy and the appeals procedure.

Although this was the lady's first visit to Britain she did not seem surprised at what I was telling her. She glanced around my office – obviously noting the crumbling plasterwork and the grubby confusion of lost property on the dresser – and said that she had already heard that the British education system was falling to pieces, but that she thought she would come and investigate for herself.

'Your teachers are always on strike aren't they?' she said, 'and I'm told they show the kids porn videos at secondary school.'

She made it quite clear that she did not intend pursuing the matter of a State education for her child and she asked me where she could get details of private schools in the city. Two prospectuses had come in that day so I scrabbled around in my waste-paper bin to find them, but as the one had become sodden with a soaking wet and bloodstained piece of cotton wool and there was a wet tea-bag sticking to the other, I suggested she just took a note of the names and telephone numbers of the headteachers.

She left my office with the information she wanted but was back again within the minute and in a very bad temper.

'How the hell do I get out of this goddamned place!' she said, and I remembered that we had a faulty latch on the main entrance door that needed a jiggling wrench on the doorknob combined with a lunge forward with a knee in order to open the door from the inside.

Having released the American lady from the school I returned to my office, made myself a mug of coffee and sat awhile thinking about what she had said. It was playtime and Miss Krantz, muffled up in a huge overcoat, long scarf and hand-knitted woolly hat, was plodding around the playground with her mug of coffee held between both hands.

The climbing frame was a wriggling mass of swinging legs, red faces and tiny gloved hands sliding about on the cold, smooth, round bars. Shabaana went streaking across the playground, her long black plaits flying out behind. Lucy, Zoe and Pip, all holding hands, raced after her. Two little boys in the shrubbery under my window had discovered a pile of leaves which they gathered to their chests in great armfuls and tried to throw over each other. Purity, with a twig, was poking at the crumbling mortar in the playground wall, and between the temporary classrooms I could see a jostling queue of boys impatiently waiting for their turn on the slider they had made across a series of frozen puddles.

The American lady hadn't liked our school and she had visited us with preconceived ideas about the British education system. It was falling to pieces she said.

Is it? I don't know . . . What do *you* think?

Postscript

Mrs Snow (in a gossipy mood recently) asked me if I had heard about the secretary at St Blogg's Primary School who had 'gone funny'. Suspicions about her state of mind were first aroused when envelopes of unaccounted-for dinner money were found stuffed behind radiators, and unopened letters from the LEA found torn up in the staff toilet.

She was often to be seen muttering to herself as she stormed down the corridor, and things finally reached a climax when she had to be forcibly restrained from stuffing a child head-first into the lost-property box. I understand that she was carried away screaming, and that she has since been declared 'sick' and recommended for early retirement.

Those of us school secretaries still holding down our jobs – having not yet been carried away screaming – have every sympathy for our sister, late of St Blogg's Primary School. In a job where one's official daily tasks can rarely be completed because of constant interruptions from teachers, children and parents, we all know that a minor frustration (like the duplicator breaking down) at the end of a day of similar frustrations is all that is needed to turn a secretary from her usual smiling self into a screeching virago who will kick the door shut in the face of the next person who tries to come in. But most of us don't react so violently. Some of us are calm, competent and serene because of inner strengths and convictions. The rest of us rely upon Valium – or reach for the bottle.

An occasion recently when I felt like kicking something (or somebody) was when I found upon my desk a cheque for the correct amount of camp money signed by one Isadora Brown. I assumed – fool that I was – that it applied to the only child going camping who had that surname. I should have known better. When the subsequent series of misunderstandings was eventually sorted out the class teacher concerned expressed surprise at my ignorance. Surely I *knew* that Isadora Brown was the mother of Wallace Pritchard, and that Alice Brown's mother was Miss Davies? In the event, I had made out a receipt for Alice Brown and handed it to her. Alice, a dim child, accepted it without comment and took it home to her mother (not so dim) who kept it. The row didn't break out until a month later when I sent Wallace home with a note asking for payment of camp money.

While a teacher in daily contact with his/her class of thirty children may be able to keep up to date with who is living with whom and under what name, a school secretary with several hundred children on file has difficulties. I once thought of creating a card-index system whereby each child's name was cross-indexed with that of his parents, but gave up this idea because of a recent trend in hyphenated surnames.

When John Townsend set up home with Angela Carruthers, the child they produced was subsequently registered at our school as Nathan Townsend-Carruthers. If this fashion continues I am most thankful that I shall have long since handed over responsibility for keeping school records by the time that Nathan Townsend-Carruthers reaches an age when he can shack up with and produce children by Felicity Berrington-Manners.

Perhaps you can now understand why school secretaries, who deal competently with dramatic events (like running out of coffee) and who react cheerfully to inconvenient ones (like a child falling head-first from

the climbing frame) may resort to outrageous behaviour or language when expected to cope with
an accumulation of petty irritations. Which brings me
to today.

It is snowing heavily. I am staring out of my office
window across the playground to another building
where, three floors up, Miss Z has her class. Miss Z
has just sent me a tin (labelled 'drawing pins') containing what appears to be dinner money, also an
envelope containing several pound coins. Jacob – who
has been sent out of Assembly for misbehaviour – is
standing in the corner picking his nose, while another
child who has just been sick and whose mother I can't
trace, sits whimpering beside me.

A man wearing a boiler suit and carrying a clipboard hovers patiently in the doorway waiting for me
to produce the key of the boiler house which I think
the caretaker has, but the caretaker has gone out. I
stare angrily at the envelope containing several pound
coins, while carrying in my head the knowledge that
Nicholas Brooks must be told not to leave school for
the Remedial Centre because his remedial teacher is
off sick; we are out of straws so I must ring the
milkman, and in five minutes' time I must switch on
the tape recorder.

I am still staring at the envelope of pound coins.
Miss Z has labelled it 'Timmy's violin money'. But
there are two Timmys in Miss Z's class – and they
both take violin lessons. And now the 'phone has
started ringing.

I can tell, by the way my one hand is gripping the
side of the desk and the other one is longing to chuck
the tin (labelled 'drawing pins') straight through the
window that I have reached that point of stress at
which a school secretary could 'go funny'. But that is
not going to be me. They will never carry *me* away
screaming because I know exactly what to do.

Over there in the corner of the office, hidden in a

box of plimsolls and bean bags underneath the photo-copier, there is a half-bottle of something strong – a drop of which in my coffee will put everything right. The difficulty is getting to the box without being seen. So what I must do is to slither off my chair like this . . . down on to my hands and knees . . . and now I must crawl underneath my table . . .

HOVEL IN THE HILLS
by Elizabeth West

A warm, funny, moving account of the simple life in rural Wales.

She was a typist. He was a mechanic. One day Elizabeth and Alan West did what many people spend a lifetime dreaming of doing – they took to the hills. *Hovel in the Hills* is the story of the first nine years of their new life in a semi-derelict farmhouse overlooking Snowdonia. It is a heart-warming and salutary tale that abounds with the joys, and the dilemmas, of opting out of the rat race.

'Mrs West writes in a lively, humorous, down-to-earth style . . . an absorbing account of a brave experiment'
Sunday Times

'I don't think I have read a better book of its kind . . . Mrs West writes remarkably well with just the right element of humour'
Daily Telegraph

'The best book I have read about getting away from it all'
Western Mail

'Conveys the joy in the countryside, in wild things and in coping for oneself'
The Times

0 552 10907 X

GARDEN IN THE HILLS
by Elizabeth West

The second enthralling book about the couple who opted out of the rate race!

Garden in the Hills is the latest account of the adventures, trials, joys and rewards of Elizabeth and Alan West's life in their farmhouse in a remote corner of Wales. In her familiarly lively style, Elizabeth West describes how they make a garden on a windswept moorland, one thousand feet above sea level, how they battle with storms, blizzards, floods and sheep and tells of their eventual success in growing herbs, fruit and vegetables. You are even invited to try some of Elizabeth's recipes – straight from her primitive but cheerful and homely kitchen!

But GARDEN IN THE HILLS ends on a rather sad note as Mrs West tells of the encroachment of the modern world that threatened to destroy their happiness.

'A moving as well as an entertaining book'
Church Times

Don't miss Elizabeth West's absorbing and humorous account of the first nine years of their isolated new life – HOVEL IN THE HILLS available from Corgi Books.

0 552 11707 2

KITCHEN IN THE HILLS
by Elizabeth West

Home-made lentil and vegetable soup with a hunk of crusty wholemeal bread ... economical and tasty brawn ... rowanberry jelly ... spicy, treacly Brown Betty ... fruit cake baked on a plate ... rhubarb gingerbread pudding ...

Here are all the recipes – some dating back to a war-time childhood – from Elizabeth West's famous Kitchen in the Hills.

All the recipes are based on the principle of making the most of what is available, using food from the hedgerow and garden and whatever is available in the larder.

Elizabeth West has produced a book which will delight all cooks and 'food browsers', and will be enjoyed by all the fans of HOVEL IN THE HILLS and GARDEN IN THE HILLS ...

0 552 12072 3

A SELECTED LIST OF
FINE AUTOBIOGRAPHIES AND BIOGRAPHIES

THE PRICES SHOWN BELOW WERE CORRECT AT THE TIME OF GOING
TO PRESS. HOWEVER TRANSWORLD PUBLISHERS RESERVE THE
RIGHT TO SHOW NEW RETAIL PRICES ON COVERS WHICH MAY
DIFFER FROM THOSE PREVIOUSLY ADVERTISED IN THE TEXT OR
ELSEWHERE.

CORGI BIOGRAPHY SERIES

☐ 99065 5	THE PAST IS MYSELF	Christabel Bielenberg	£3.50
☐ 99271 2	MY HAPPY DAYS IN HELL	George Faludy	£4.95
☐ 12833 3	THE HOUSE BY THE DVINA	Eugenie Fraser	£3.95
☐ 12863 5	THE LONG JOURNEY HOME	Flora Leipman	£3.95
☐ 99247 X	THE FORD OF HEAVEN	Brian Power	£3.50
☐ 99293 3	THE PUPPET EMPEROR	Brian Power	£3.95

GENERAL AUTOBIOGRAPHIES & BIOGRAPHIES

☐ 12851 1	CHILDRENS HOSPITAL	Peggy Anderson	£3.99
☐ 09332 7	GO ASK ALICE	Anonymous	£2.50
☐ 13220 9	THE GENTLE ART: A MIDWIFE'S STORY		£3.95
		Penny Armstrong & Sheryl Fieldman	
☐ 99054 X	BORSTAL BOY	Brendan Behan	£4.50
☐ 99307 7	QADDAFI	David Blundy & Andrew Lycett	£4.00
☐ 12889 9	ADRIFT	Steven Callahan	£2.95
☐ 99328 X	THATCHER'S BRITAIN	Terry Coleman	£3.95
☐ 13126 1	CATHERINE COOKSON COUNTRY	Catherine Cookson	£5.95
☐ 09373 4	OUR KATE	Catherine Cookson	£2.95
☐ 11772 2	'H' THE AUTOBIOGRAPHY OF A CHILD PROSTITUTE AND HEROIN ADDICT	Christiane F.	£2.50
☐ 12727 2	MEN	Anna Ford	£2.95
☐ 12501 6	BEYOND THE HIGHLAND LINE	Richard Frere	£1.95
☐ 13070 2	BORN LUCKY. AN AUTOBIOGRAPHY	John Francome	£2.95
☐ 13254 3	ANNE FRANK REMEMBERED	Miep Gies & Alison Leslie Gold	£2.95
☐ 13032 X	NO LAUGHING MATTER	Joseph Heller	£2.95
☐ 99285 2	GETTING HITLER INTO HEAVEN	John Graven Hughes	£4.95
☐ 13248 9	CUTTING THE LION'S TAIL	Mohamed Heikal	£4.50
☐ 13060 5	KHASHOGGI: THE STORY OF THE WORLD'S RICHEST MAN	Ron Kessler	£3.95
☐ 99294 1	TO HELL AND BACK	Nikki Lauda	£2.95
☐ 99158 9	BRENDAN BEHAN	Ulick O'Connor	£2.95
☐ 99143 0	CELTIC DAWN	Ulick O'Connor	£4.95
☐ 13094 X	WISEGUY	Nicholas Pileggi	£2.95
☐ 12577 6	PLACE OF STONES	Ruth Janette Ruck	£2.50
☐ 13058 3	THE MARILYN CONSPIRACY	Milo Speriglio	£2.50
☐ 12589 X	AND I DON'T WANT TO LIVE THIS LIFE	Deborah Spungen	£3.50
☐ 12072 3	KITCHEN IN THE HILLS	Elizabeth West	£2.50
☐ 11707 2	GARDEN IN THE HILLS	Elizabeth West	£2.50
☐ 10907 X	HOVEL IN THE HILLS	Elizabeth West	£2.50